SRIDEVI

Amborish Roychoudhury is a National Award-winning writer, biographer and film historian. His first book, *In A Cult of Their Own: Bollywood Beyond Box-Office*, won a Special Mention at the 66th National Film Awards. He has written for *Outlook*, *Firstpost*, *Filmfare*, *Huffpost*, *MUBI Notebook* and the *Free Press Journal*, among others. This will be his second published book.

SRIDEVI

THE SOUTH YEARS

AMBORISH ROYCHOUDHURY

RUPA

Published by
Rupa Publications India Pvt. Ltd 2023
7/16, Ansari Road, Daryaganj
New Delhi 110002

Sales centres:
Prayagraj Bengaluru Chennai
Hyderabad Jaipur Kathmandu
Kolkata Mumbai

P-ISBN: 978-93-5702-462-4
E-ISBN: 978-93-5702-460-0

First impression 2023

10 9 8 7 6 5 4 3 2 1

The moral right of the author has been asserted.

Printed in India

*To Amitabh Bachchan, who has shaped my life
and career in ways he will never know.*

Contents

Foreword
by Kamal Haasan

Whenever I think of Sridevi, I think of a child. I wasn't much older either. But I found her innocence worthy of exploration and training. She had that quality, something the Japanese call *shoshin*, which means the open mind of a student willing to learn. I was a child artist myself, and we were brought up in a celluloid cage. We were parrots. We could say things, repeat things they didn't expect us to say. So that's what it was. I understood it and I passed it on to her.

People who watched our films always thought that we were either lovers or wannabe lovers or a could-have-been couple. None of it, of course, was true. Till the end, she kept calling me 'sir'. She even called me 'sir' when I was 19. There was a reason for that. Mr Balachander (KB), our mentor, gave me the responsibility of rehearsing her. I was equally naive, but I was a senior student. I was like the student who is made to run the class while the teacher is away. But then they always come and take over.

I was sort of the student leader among the Balachander protégés, so I was a much hated man. KB sir would ask me to rehearse the rest of the actors while he was away doing something else. He used to say things which seemed rude at times, but then he was our teacher; he gave us life. We can't complain. He was fond of me. He used to tell Sridevi and all other actors, 'Watch this fellow perform. Why can't you do like that?' Which was a bad comparison. No one should do it. But Sridevi didn't mind at all. If you gave her logic, she would set aside her ego. But you have to explain the logic. Mr Shekhar Kapur is a brilliant man. I respect him a lot. We never thought of making a film together but we have discussed so many stories. He once said to me, 'This Sridevi... She is a bag of tricks! What more does a director want? Do you have another bag?' So there she was, arranging her acting wares in front of you. All you had to do was choose.

I was a choreographer too. I had worked as an assistant choreographer with Mr Thangappan. And in the early days, Sridevi couldn't dance at all. She was very conscious about her feet. And I used to tell her that it doesn't matter. That is the kind of relationship I shared with Sridevi. It is very strange to talk about it now. It is like saying that John Wayne was bald. It doesn't matter. John Wayne was John Wayne.

She used to be very nervous as an actor in the early days. Maybe because she was a learner. Whatever she did used to seem very embarrassing to her. I had been through that, so I understood. We used to have conversations about it. She was my understudy and I made no bones about it. I was not kind. I am one of those teachers who are not kind. I had to knuckle her on the head—in Tamil we call it 'Kuttu'. When you are trying to teach a sister or a younger sibling and they make a mistake, you knuckle them on top of their head. That was the relationship between me and Sridevi. It is very difficult to explain.

She was petrified of injections. I used to run around whenever we had a hospital sequence. I used to pick up a syringe and run around, saying that I have this and I now must give you this injection. I used to run around chasing her and her mother, Mrs Rajeswari, used to intervene.

When she was maybe 17 or 19, she used to sit on her mother's lap at lunch time and her mother used to feed her. Her mother would pick up a morsel and stuff it into her mouth. I used to make fun of this excessive pampering. I remember telling her that mothers always die before the daughters so she better learn to eat on her own. And how she cried! These are the moments I remember.

I thought I had better experience than her so I decided to teach her. But actually, I myself had very limited knowledge back then. Though that didn't mean that I couldn't play the pompous teacher! But she was a humble student, and a very obedient actor.

I think the last time I met her was at an award ceremony in Mumbai. If I remember correctly, it was a couple of months before she died. Her husband was there, and I was there. We had just watched a footage of ours. She hugged me and wouldn't let go. I was surprised. She hugged me tight and that is the last I saw of her. That is Sridevi. She might have had a short life, but it was a magnificent one nevertheless.

To me Sridevi was not just a dear friend and a respected colleague, but also someone I considered family. We shared an artistic kinship that transcended the boundaries of the silver screen. I may have schooled her but I was only her school teacher. She earned her PhD with the help of a greater teacher, her humility. But it was a great relationship which even some marriages don't have. She was my darling, she was my child and that's how I thought of her.

Amborish Roychoudhury's book on Sridevi's journey through South Indian cinema provides a much-needed window into her extraordinary body of work. I wish him all the best and hope that Sridevi fans won't pass up this opportunity to delve into her films all over again.

Foreword
by Baradwaj Rangan

It is difficult to capture any life within the two covers of a book, and the task becomes doubly difficult when the life is that of an actor like Sridevi. How do you open up to the reader the inner workings of someone who never opened up to anyone? Directors sometimes talk about how Sridevi was a bundle of energy on sets, especially in articles that have surfaced after her too-early demise. However, on-record interviews with her are scarce and even if you find them, they yield little. It's almost as if she was an equally proficient actor with the media—she knew how to speak to them without really, you know, speaking to them. According to most accounts, Sridevi had become more sociable in her 'Bombay days' than in her reign over Tamil and Telugu cinema. Still, the gaps are many and the insights few.

It is, then, left to the scribe to put together this famously enigmatic jigsaw puzzle. *Sridevi: The South Years*, is about Sridevi's work in Tamil, Telugu, Malayalam and Kannada cinema—the places where she learnt to crawl, walk and soar before the camera. There are many, including me, who claim that Sridevi was better utilized as an actor in the South than she was in the Hindi film industry. Down south, she was an actor-star. Then, she went to Mumbai and became a star-actor. And yes, there is a difference. An actor-star is someone whose roles come first. With a star-actor, their persona comes first. Neither category is 'better'. Each one is just a different approach, and very few performers become an actor-star as well as a star-actor.

The author—or should we call him 'detective'—Amborish Roychoudhury has spoken to a number of sources to try and solve the mystery that is Sridevi. In the absence of her own words, we get words from others who observed her on sets both before and after the director called 'action'. The person who emerges from this research, while still a mystery, makes things a little clearer. At least some of the fog is lifted. The 'real Sridevi' may never be revealed to the public. There was a running joke in the Hindi film press that every question one asked her was answered with the same two words: 'ask Mummy'. But the actor we get to glimpse in this book is a good substitute. Thanks to Amborish Roychoudhury, we no longer have to wonder. We no longer have to...'ask Mummy'.

Baradwaj Rangan
Film critic and editor-in-chief, Galatta Plus

Introduction

This book began its journey as a conventional Sridevi biography. That's what I set about to write. *What a great book it will be,* I thought. I mapped it all out. A series of interviews with her co-stars and directors in Mumbai, a few customary visits to the National Film Archives of India, revisiting all her films twice over and then, the part I was most excited about—a trip down south to explore her roots. And then, it all began to unravel.

Nobody was ready to talk. I reached out to some of the veterans who had worked with her. No response from them. After about a dozen WhatsApp messages and a bunch of unreturned calls, I was able to talk to Boney Kapoor on a couple of occasions. He didn't think, at that time, that a biography was a great idea. Not one to lose heart, I took a trip to Chennai. I tried, with my very limited resources, to reach out to those closest to her. But there again, I hit an insurmountable brick wall. It was then, while I was in Chennai, that I started exploring her work in South India before she came to Hindi films. And boy, was I hooked.

K. Balachander's *Moondru Mudichu* was the first South film of hers that I watched. There was a subtitled copy on YouTube. I was blown away. For a film buff who grew up watching her Hindi films, this was a fascinating experience.

Was she really playing Rajinikanth's mother? I thought. And
then I came across Bharathiraja's *Pathinaru Vayathinile*. Both
these films had Sridevi starring alongside Kamal Haasan
and Rajinikanth in their early days. This was nothing like
the Sridevi I knew! She was a completely different actor,
who seemed like she was trying to find her voice and doing
very unconventional and risqué roles. As I kept walking
further and further down this road, I realized this could
potentially be a whole new book. I started to watch more
of her Tamil, Telugu and Malayalam films. Most of them
were available online, with or without subtitles. But after a
point, the subtitles stopped mattering to me. With a little
help from fellow film buffs and friends who speak these
languages, I was able to progress through her seemingly
endless filmography in the South.

I tried my best to meet Bharathiraja, the awe-inspiring
director of *Pathinaru Vayathinile, Sigappu Rojakkal* and *Solva
Sawan*. I went up to his film school, the Bharathiraja
International Institute of Cinema, met his manager and
spent a good couple of hours waiting for him to show up.
This happened on two different occasions, after which I gave
up. Nothing much was happening on the biography, but as
I was in Chennai I met as many experts as I could to get
some context on her work in Tamil cinema. I met producer,
writer, columnist and film historian G. Dhananjayan; actor and
writer Mohan Raman; journalist, actor and filmmaker Chitra
Lakshmanan; actor, theatre personality and K. Balachander's
protégé Kavithalayaa Krishnan; and finally, film critic and
writer Baradwaj Rangan. I spoke to them extensively about
her Tamil films, their place in Tamil cinema and her equation
with the then two up-and-coming actors—Rajinikanth and
Kamal Haasan—who went on to sit on the throne of the
Tamil film industry much like she did.

Eventually, I also spoke to Telugu movie critic Jalapathy Gudelli. With Malayalam cinema, I had drawn a blank till then. I tried to reach out to movie critics and academicians from Kerala to talk about Sridevi's Malayalam films. But most of them, at least the ones I spoke to, seemed to have the impression that her works in Malayalam were not worthy of mention, unremarkable or too few to talk about. Most of them couldn't recollect any of her films. However, what I later found about her work in the Malayalam film industry was just as intriguing as the other industries. I have tried to address this in the chapters that talk about Malayalam cinema.

While all of this was going on, two Sridevi biographies came out in quick succession. One of them was much publicized and launched in a big way. By this time, I was on a different trip altogether. Obviously, writing a conventional biography didn't make sense anymore and that was a good thing too. This book could now become a thing of its own. What intrigued me was this long, undisturbed span of 28 years (1969–1997) in which Sridevi worked non-stop in multiple film industries. There wasn't a single year in this period when she wasn't working. She's probably the only actor whom we saw grow from toddler to teenager to adolescent and then to a woman—and cinema was witness to it all.

The other thing that interested me was how Hindi cinema allowed her to merely be a dancing diva who could show a range of histrionics. *Chandni* and *Lamhe* was the most they thought she could do. She was absolutely brilliant in *Mr India*, *ChaalBaaz* and similar films but they didn't really push her boundaries. The 1980s, when she joined Bollywood, was a terrible phase for popular Hindi cinema. Towards the end of the decade, there were those who were sounding the death knell of Hindi films altogether. G.P.

Sippy had said to a popular magazine that his grandchildren will never be in the business and that it will die out soon.[1] Only the blue-collar workers and the working classes were frequenting the cinema theatres which had become shanty, stinking and unwelcome places. Hence, films were essentially manufactured to cater to that kind of sensibility.

In this environment—though Sridevi was headlining films that were great money-spinners—most of the projects that she was offered neither had the kind of scripts or characterizations, nor the kind of co-actors that she was accustomed to in the South. She was paired with Amitabh Bachchan only thrice. She co-starred with Dilip Kumar in a rather weak film, and in another blockbuster where they didn't have a lot of scenes together. But in South Indian cinema, she got to lock horns with the likes of Sivaji Ganesan, M.G. Ramachandran (MGR), Gemini Ganesan, Akkineni Nageswara Rao (ANR), N.T. Rama Rao (NTR), Ghattamaneni Siva Rama Krishna Murthy (popularly known as Superstar Krishna), J. Jayalalithaa, Anjali Devi, Sankaramanchi Janaki (popularly known as Sowcar Janaki) and Manorama along with Rajinikanth, Kamal Haasan, Chiranjeevi, Nagarjuna, Venkatesh and other such legends. These associations were not restricted to just one or two films, but scores of movies over the years. She had worked with them, learned from them and, in her own way, upstaged them when her time came.

And that is the germ of the idea behind this book— to cover her work in South Indian cinema in four major languages: Tamil, Telugu, Malayalam and Kannada. The book begins with her stepping into the world of cinema as

---

[1]Mitra, Sumit, 'Indian Film Industry Faces Its Biggest Ever Crisis with Advent of Video and Television, Changing Audience Tastes', *India Today*, 31 December 1985, https://tinyurl.com/5xj7zm7t. Accessed on 24 May 2023.

a six-year-old with *Thunaivan* (Tamil) and ends with her last South Indian film as a lead actor, *S.P. Parasuram* (Telugu). This is not an account of her life in any shape or form. It will just talk about the incredible films she did in these industries, before Bollywood beckoned. For the diehard Sridevi fan who has only seen her Hindi films, this book intends to be a primer to get to know the 'other' Sridevi and dozens of her incredible films they never got to see.

In the course of writing this book, I had plenty of help. I am deeply thankful to G. Dhananjayan, Mohan Raman, Chitra Lakshmanan, Kavithalayaa Krishnan, Jalapathy Gudelli and Baradwaj Rangan for their priceless inputs. Their insights have enriched the book immensely. I am also deeply indebted to Jitesh Pillai, without whose help and encouragement much of my writing wouldn't see the light of day.

My friend and partner-in-most-crimes, Prasanna Raman, was a major force behind the book. He made a lot of things happen and his knowledge of Tamil language and cinema was a huge asset for me. It was he who managed to speak to Nellai Sundar Rajan, a publicist from the heydays of Tamil cinema. Sundar Rajan does not speak any other language except Tamil, and Prasanna swung into action and grabbed some insights from him which I have infused into the book. Through my friend and ex-colleague Rajagopal Prabhakar, I was able to connect with Kaushik Ramaswamy who was an invaluable help in securing many of the interviews, especially those of Baradwaj Rangan and G. Dhananjayan. I am eternally grateful to both. The episodes of the Telugu TV show *Soundaryalahari*, which had interviews of Sridevi, K. Raghavendra Rao and Ram Gopal Varma were translated by Rahul Kurup. I must also thank my friends Ganesh Prabhakar and Padmanabhan Nair for their invaluable help with plot summaries of some of the Tamil and Malayalam films, respectively. Ganesh was also of great help in transcribing some of the interviews. My ex-colleague Sushanth Ashok's mother, Shalini Ashok, was kind enough to translate a summary of *Soundaryalahari* for me. A special mention needs to be made of Stills Gnanam, a collector of rare photographs and memorabilia who provided me with the photographs and stills used in this book. The word 'stills' attached to his name is a reference to the important work he is doing of preserving and disseminating stills of old South Indian films to journalists, researchers and film historians. Thanks to Mohan Raman and Prasanna Raman for putting me in touch with him. Prasanna also helped me communicate with Gnanam, who speaks only Tamil.

Thanks to Baradwaj Rangan and Jitesh Pillai for helping me get in touch with Kamal Haasan. I owe a debt to Kamal Haasan who found time from his busy schedule to put his thoughts down for the foreword. I owe a debt of thanks to Monisha Ravi from Mr Haasan's team as well. A million thanks to Vaibhav Vishal, who very graciously reached out to Ram Gopal Varma on my behalf. Heartfelt gratitude to Ram Gopal Varma for allowing me to use his perspective in the book.

I would like to end this introduction with a final word on languages and cultural nuances. I am a Bengali film buff who mostly writes about Hindi cinema. Like any self-respecting film enthusiast, I watch plenty of films in languages that I don't speak thanks to subtitles. I have watched all the films spoken about in this book and employed all my faculties to try and capture their essence. But I have no knowledge of these languages nor do I claim to understand the cultural mores of these traditions. If I have missed any important films, or misinterpreted the nuances, meaning or sensitivity at any point; I record my apologies in advance—especially to the film buffs and viewers who belong to these cultures.

Happy reading!

Part I

Her Story

One

It All Began with a
Love Story

A story as epic and enigmatic as the early years of
Sridevi's career deserves a prologue as mythical and
fantastical as her films were back then. Much like
those films this origin is a mixture of truth, myth and hearsay.
As with all great stories, this one also begins with two
strangers falling in love. Right around the time our great
nation was in the throes of independence Katari Venkataswami
Reddy was plying buses from Tirupati, the temple city of
Andhra Pradesh. It was at the time a part of the Madras
state. Reddy ran buses along the Tirupati–Garapalli–
Jammalamadugu route. Jammalamadugu was a quaint
old town, nestled in the centre of the state. It was in this
sleepy town that Katari Venkataswami Reddy met Venkata
Ratnamma, who was then employed as a medical attendant
at one of the hospitals of Jammalamadugu.

Cupid struck, and it was only a matter of time before
Katari Venkataswami Reddy and Venkata Ratnamma tied
the knot. Following their marriage, Reddy sought greener
pastures and suddenly his work in transportation didn't seem
adequate as there were more mouths to feed. Like his wife,

he too bagged a job at a hospital. The couple were parents to six beautiful children: Balasubramaniyam, Rajeswaramma, Subbaramayya, Anasuayamma, Amrutamma and Shantamma. Little did they know that one of their daughters would go on to birth a girl who would have a massive cultural impact on the Indian film industries.

Rajeswaramma or Rajeswari was different from the other kids. Unlike her siblings, she was ambitious. From her earliest days, she wanted to become an actress. And unlike most girls who wanted to become an actress, she did eventually fulfil her dream in a way.

When the eldest son, Balasubramaniyam, decided to shift to Chennai (then Madras) the family followed him. It was most likely during her sojourn in Madras that Rajeswari got a shot at her dream. But instead of Tamil, she was seen more often in Telugu films. 1950s and '60s were interesting times in the cinema of South India. Films in the four languages—Tamil, Telugu, Malayalam and Kannada—were all being made in Madras in the early days. Eventually, they moved to their respective home states but that took a while. In fact, Telugu cinema completely shifted its base to Hyderabad only in the late 1980s and early 1990s. One of the earliest films made after the shift was Ram Gopal Varma's *Siva* (1989). In this melting pot of dialects and languages that Madras was back then, Rajeswari found her way into Telugu films.

Not much is known about Rajeswari's work as an actress. Online sources, like IMDb, do not list her filmography. The earliest film one can see her in is a Telugu film called *Chivaraku Migiledi* (1960). The film was a remake of the Bengali hit *Deep Jwele Jaai* (1959). It is unclear whether the film was Rajeswari's debut, but she appeared in a song in the movie which is still quite popular. The song was

'Andaniki Andam Nene'. It is an elaborate dance number, where Rajeswari is seen dancing on the stage before a live audience while mouthing the lyrics. While the movie is all but forgotten, the song still gets old-timers misty-eyed. The film featured the song 'Sudhavol Suhasini', an exact replica of the Bengali 'Ei Raat Tomar Amar', later reproduced in Hindi as 'Ye Nayan Dare Dare' for an unrelated film called *Kohraa* (1964). *Chivaraku Migiledi/ Deep Jwele Jaai* was remade in Hindi as *Khamoshi* (1969).

It was a blink-and-you-miss-it role and Rajeswari didn't get a lot of offers following this. But there were a couple of actors who did take notice. One of them was Kanta Rao. In the 1960s, Telugu cinema was primarily dominated by the histrionics of three actors: ANR, NTR and Kanta Rao. Kanta Rao's birth-name was Tadepalli Lakshmi Kanta Rao. He was known for his swashbuckling roles and characters in films like *Lava Kusa* (1963), *Pandava Vanavasam* (1965) and *Mutyala Muggu* (1975). Rao spotted Rajeswari in the *Chivaraku Migiledi* song, and was floored by her beauty and charm. He was impressed enough to recommend her for one of his upcoming projects, *Shanti Nivasam* (1960), co-starring ANR. But despite the stellar cast and more screen time than she was used to (she played the sister of the heroine, Krishna Kumari), the film didn't do much for Rajeswari's career.

The other actor who was enamoured by her was Ranga Rao, a small-time Telugu movie actor. Not much is known about him other than this particular titbit. Ranga and Rajeswari exchanged vows and got married sometime around 1960. But Ranga didn't have an established career, which may have put his ability to provide for his family under the scanner. Very soon, fault lines appeared in the marriage. And this was where the seeds of our grand saga were sown. If Rajeswari and Ranga Rao had managed a blissful conjugal life, we probably wouldn't have had *Mr India*, *Sadma*, *ChalBaaz*, *Chandni* or *Pathinaru Vayathinile.* We wouldn't have had Sridevi.

While Rajeswari was having second thoughts about matrimony, the man she was destined to spend her life with was charting his own course. To the rest of India, Sivakasi is known for the firecrackers it produces. In the unlikely eventuality that you do burn a cracker in the near future, do take a good look at the package before you throw it away. 'Made in Sivakasi' will be etched somewhere quietly in the corner. It was this Sivakasi that K. Ayyappan Naidu called his home.

Ayyappan was a lawyer from Sivakasi who was born into a family of politicians, a profession he himself entered begrudgingly many years later. But it was his practice of law that put him on the same course as Rajeswari, his future wife. It is said that Rajeswari was looking for a way out of her marriage with Ranga Rao when she met Ayyappan, her divorce lawyer. Destiny then took some delightful turns for them.

It was fate that brought Rajeswari and Ayyappan together. Both of them had been married before. He even had a son from the earlier marriage, Satish (who played his own role in Sridevi's life and career later). Ayyappan and Rajeswari were finally married at Sivakasi. The union of a single father and a divorcee might not have gone down without any opposition. But their families relented and the wedding took place at Sivakasi in the early 1960s. The couple then embarked on a new life in Ayyappan's native village, Meenampatti, barely 5 km from Sivakasi.

It was here, at Meenampatti, that Shree Amma Yanger Ayyappan—the angel we know as Sridevi—was born on 13 August 1963. Soon, the family moved to Madras where the seeds of Sridevi's acting life were sown.

Two

Sowing the Seeds

Three men were responsible for Sridevi being launched in films: a kingmaker, a poet and a 'muscle man'. Of course, they had no idea what they were putting in motion or that they were turning the wheels of Indian cinema's future. Who could have known that the little girl before them would later set a million hearts ablaze?

The Poet

Notwithstanding the giants of Hindi/Urdu poetry roaming the jungles of Bollywood back then, the first man to win the National Film Award for best lyrics (when it was first instituted in 1969) wasn't a Hindi film lyricist. It was the great Tamil poet, Kannadasan, revered as Kaviarasu or Kavirajar in Tamil Nadu. Some believe him to be the greatest Tamil poet after the legendary C. Subramania Bharathi.

He can unequivocally be called the greatest Tamil movie lyricist. A hedonist in thought and spirit, Kannadasan was known to down a few drinks and put pen to paper as the most exquisite words flowed out and formed poetry. He was known to turn up on the sets too drunk to stand straight, but when the situation for a song was explained to him he would manically scribble his lines like a man possessed and come up with some of the most sublime songs ever composed. Tamil film buffs swear by his lyrics as much as they swear by Ilaiyaraaja's music.

The Kingmaker

Like all great Tamil movie legends, Kannadasan had overt political leanings and hobnobbed with some popular politicians of the time. One of them was Kumaraswami 'Kingmaker' Kamaraj. The man was called kingmaker for a reason. Kamaraj was the president of the Indian National Congress when Jawaharlal Nehru passed away. He turned down an offer to be the prime minister himself, and enabled Lal Bahadur Shastri to be elevated to that position. Similarly on Shastri's demise, it was Kamaraj who was instrumental in Indira Gandhi stepping into his shoes. In January 1966, the then United States (US) Vice President Hubert Humphrey said Kamaraj was 'one of the greatest political leaders in all the countries of the free world'.[1]

The dynamic between Kannadasan and Kamaraj is interesting enough to merit a film of its own. When the two had a fight and weren't on talking terms, Kannadasan wrote a message to him through a song in the film *Pattanathil Bhootham* (1967) which roughly translates to, 'Ask Sivagami's son if (and when) I can join him again.' Kamaraj's mother was called Sivagami. When Kamaraj was about to be elected as Tamil Nadu's chief minister, Kannadasan wrote a song celebrating his win. When Kamaraj was getting cold feet

---

[1] Chhibber, Maneesh, 'K. Kamaraj: The Southern Stalwart Who Gave India Two PMs', *The Print*, 2 October 2018, https://tinyurl.com/4bfcuwk4. Accessed on 24 May 2023.

about going to the United Nations (UN) because he didn't know English, the poet composed a song urging him to move forward come what may. All of this exchange, mind you, was happening via films songs.

This was in or around 1968. Ayyappan and Rajeswari were raising a happy little family while finding a way to adjust to the hustle and bustle of Madras. Sridevi was a sensitive child, often lost in a world of her own. It was easy to peg her as an introvert because she was so withdrawn, but there were rare moments when the future performer peeked out of her. She narrated one such incident in an interview, almost 20 years later:

> Always frightened I'd react to the smallest noise with a start. Always found trailing my mother, holding her sari pallu in my mouth. I don't know when and how things changed. An unreasonable childhood memory is of me dining at a restaurant. Suddenly I stopped eating, got up from my chair, walked to the dais where the band was playing and started dancing. I remember I wouldn't stop dancing till my father pulled me away and brought me back to my chair. My family must have been awfully embarrassed watching me go berserk. But I was too young to know what I was doing.[2]

This phenomenon would always be a part of her life and work. Throughout her career as a heroine she mostly kept to herself, socializing only when absolutely necessary. But the very second she faced the camera, a floodgate of energy opened that electrified the whole atmosphere. When the shot was done, she used to clam up again.

Back in the 1960s, Sridevi and her family were living

---

[2]Somaaya, Bhawana, *Take 25: Star Insights & Attitudes*, Sambhav Publishers, 2002.

in the CIT Colony in Mylapore. Ayyappan, like his brother and his family, had to make an entry into politics. It all boiled down to choosing a party. His brother was already a senior member of the Janata Party. Ayyappan, on the other hand, closely followed the exploits of the Congress and its leader K. Kamaraj. In those days, Ayyappan used to visit the Kamaraj residence at Thirumalai Pillai Road quite often.

On one such evening, he may have taken his daughter along. Little Sridevi was delighted at the opportunity of going out with her father. When they reached Kamaraj's residence, he was surrounded by his associates discussing the possible reasons for his recent defeat in his constituency (Virudhunagar). Ayyappan, eager to learn the ropes of politics was quickly sucked into the discussion as well.

As the elders spoke the Greek and Latin of politics, little Sridevi was bored to bits. Her initial exuberance of going out with her father was replaced with monotony. She was roaming about the hall, gazing at the pictures of Indian political icons lining the walls. But how was that going to hold her attention for long?

She was getting impatient. She tugged at her father's clothes and asked if they could go now. That was when the cherubic little kid caught the kingmaker's attention. Ayyappan grinned from ear to ear and introduced her as his daughter. Kamaraj wanted to know about her schooling. Ayyappan revealed she would be turning five soon and they wanted to put her in for dance and music training, since her mother wanted her to become an actress. 'That's fine,' said Kamaraj, 'but don't stop schooling her.'

Kamaraj turned to his poet friend, who was observing from a distance and smiling away. 'Help this cute child, if you can.' The Kaviarasu nodded his approval.[3] That day, they left Kamaraj's house and headed home brimming with promise and potential.

Rajeswari was eager thinking that her daughter had found her way into the movies, much like herself. Kannadasan too was enamoured with the child's angelic face and convinced she would cause some flutter on-screen. All he had to do was to reach out to a producer. Enter Marudur Marudachalamurthy Ayyavoo (M.M.A.) 'Sandow' Chinnappa Thevar, the 'muscle man' I mentioned at the very start.

The Muscle Man

M.M.A. Chinnappa Thevar (Devar) was given the moniker 'Sandow' early on due to his immensely muscular frame (reference to Eugen Sandow, the first celebrity bodybuilder the world had ever known). One of the most successful producers of Tamil cinema, he founded Thevar Films (or Devar Films) and was probably best known for his films showcasing animals in significant parts. There was no PETA (People for the Ethical Treatment of Animals) in those days, and you could make animals perform all sorts of ungodly acrobatics on-screen. The most iconic of these was a Hindi film, *Haathi Mere Saathi*, which Thevar painstakingly mounted and executed with Rajesh Khanna in the lead. It was during this phase of planning to make his first Hindi film that Kannadasan got in touch with him to cast the toddler.

Thevar was known for being a devoted worshipper of Lord Muruga, an immensely popular deity especially in Tamil Nadu. Around the time he met Sridevi, he was making a

[3]Narayanan, Maalan, 'The Girl with a Halo', *Open*, 28 February 2018, https://tinyurl.com/mjnt33ny. Accessed on 8 June 2023.

movie featuring his favourite deity. Thevar was planning
Thunaivan, a devotional film that revolved around a devotee
of Lord Muruga. When Thevar set his eyes on the child,
he knew he'd found his Muruga. He advised Ayyappan to
meet M.A. Thirumugam, the director of the film and also
Sandow's younger brother, and it wasn't long before Sridevi
was playing the role of a child Muruga in *Thunaivan* (1969).

The Birth of a Star

Sridevi's few minutes on-screen were glorious. The film can
be found on YouTube. A close look at the scene puts one
in awe of the six-year-old Sridevi's histrionics. Tell me you
can't see the spark that was to later consume the whole
nation, unabated for 30 years!

Despite appearing at the fag end of the movie, Sridevi
stole the show. It was as if she knew what she was born to
do. There was not a moment of dithering or the natural
timidity you see in the eyes of a child in an unfamiliar
environment. In those six minutes, she had conquered
the world of cinema. The audience was enraptured by
the toddler portraying their revered Lord Muruga. Sridevi
had, for all intents and purposes, truly arrived. All the
posters and publicity material of the film featured her
prominently. She wasn't a star yet, but it was obvious that
she was special.

In her very first film, Sridevi had her brush with stars.
In this film, her co-stars were Sowcar Janaki and A.V.M.
Rajan. Sowcar Janaki was a major star across Tamil, Telugu
and Kannada film industries. South Indian film fans have a
long tradition of prefixing stars' names with titles of their
films. This includes the contemporary Kannada film star
Kichcha Sudeep (named after his character Kichcha from

the film *Huchcha*) and Tamil star Jayam Ravi, named after his debut film *Jayam* (2003). Sowcar Janaki was named thus due to the popularity of her Telugu film *Shavukaru* (1950). Henceforward, she came to be credited as Shavukaru Janaki in Telugu films and as Sowcar Janaki in her Tamil work. In a 1985 interview given to Bhawana Somaaya, Sridevi reminisced about meeting Sowcar Janaki for the first time:

> [...] At the shooting, I saw Sowcar Janaki. I liked her shimmery clothes and jewellery. My first film was shot inside a temple. I played Lord Murugan. Just before the shot, the director insisted that I shave my head to play the role of the deity. My mother wasn't willing. 'My child has to go to school,' she cried.
>
> There were long discussions. Eventually, Sowcar Janaki intervened and suggested I wear a wig. The wig felt funny on the head. Nevertheless, I thoroughly enjoyed myself in the film atmosphere.[4]

Close on the heels of *Thunaivan* came a plethora of mythological films, with Sridevi as the quintessential Muruga for Tamil filmgoers. This includes films like *Aathi Parasakthi* (1971) and *Agathiyar* (1972).

These three men—Kingmaker Kamaraj, the poet Kannadasan and 'Sandow' Chinnappa Thevar—laid the foundation for Sridevi's stardom. Had they not seen the face of a god in her that day, the world would probably not have witnessed the phenomenon called Sridevi.

Kingmaker Kumaraswami Kamaraj passed away in 1975, having 'made' two of India's most famous prime ministers as well as one of the greatest female stars in Bollywood's firmament. His poet friend, Kannadasan, died soon after

---

[4]Ibid.

composing the lyrics for a film called *Moondram Pirai* (1982) which starred a grown-up Sridevi. *Moondram Pirai* (1982) was remade in Hindi the very next year as *Sadma* (1983).

Three

The Art of Playing God

Decades before she became a film goddess, Sridevi was playing a god on-screen and the South Indian moviegoing audience was eating out of her hands. I do not use the term 'South Indian' loosely like we often tend to do. As is evident from the previous chapter, Sridevi played child gods and demi-gods in a bevy of Tamil, Malayalam as well as Kannada movies. Owing to her sweeping success as Lord Muruga in her Tamil debut, *Thunaivan*, Sridevi was flooded with offers to play deities in film after film.

She played Muruga in films like *Kumara Sambhavam, Aathi Parasakthi* and *Agathiyar*. *Kumara Sambhavam* was multilingual. It was also shot in Malayalam where she was Subramanian, the same deity who's referred to as Muruga in Tamil. She also appeared as Krishna in a Tamil film, *Agathiyar*.

It was like an invisible door had been flung open all of a sudden. Close on the heels of Tamil and Malayalam hits, the Telugu film industry beckoned her too. In those days, even as a child, Sridevi had a quality in her act that would immediately grasp everyone's attention. Similar to her first performance as Muruga, all her subsequent roles sparkled with a level of authenticity and comfort which demonstrated that even she believed that this is what she was born to do. Thevar and his brother, Thirumugam, were quite the team. Thevar was the producer, while Thirumugam mounted the director's chair. For about two decades, they worked in film after film. Most of these were with Tamil cinema's greatest superstar (before Rajinikanth came along), Maruthur Gopalan Ramachandran or MGR as his devotees call him. Thevar and Thirumugam made some 16 films with MGR as the lead, and some 20 other films with other actors. *Thunaivan* was one of many such films.

Like most Tamilians who are religiously inclined, Thevar was quite obsessed with the stories of Lord Muruga and his exploits. He was known to donate a huge part of his bounty from the box-office collection of his films to Muruga temples. In the middle of shooting he would start praying, mumbling his entreaties to the deity, asking him to ensure that the shot goes well. He made some four films with Lord Muruga at the centre: *Deivam, Thiruvarul, Murugan Adimai* and *Thunaivan*. Legend has it that during a raid of his house by the income tax department, officials ran into countless packets of *vibhooti* (consecrated ash) from Muruga temples. If on a cloudy day he needed the sun to be out during shootings, Thevar would look skyward and yell, '*Dei Muruga veyila viduda* (Muruga, let the sun out)!'

Muruga is an extremely popular deity in the Tamil pantheon of gods. The deity is akin to how Ganesha is in Maharashtra or Durga/Kali is in West Bengal. Muruga, also known as Kartikeya or Subramanian, is the son of Shiva and Parvati and the sibling of Ganesha. According to legends, it was Muruga who instructed the sage Agathiyar (known as Agastya Rishi in the rest of India) to create the Tamil language.

Like his brother Ganesha, Muruga has been worshipped

as a child god. Muruga has been portrayed countless times on-screen, with actors like Master Sridhar and Sridevi playing the roles. Both of them apparently played the role of the deity in a film called *Kandhan Karunai* (1967). I won't dwell much on this, as the details are not etched out too well. On multiple online platforms, it is *Kandhan Karunai* that's been stated as Sridevi's movie debut. But if one looks closely, the child actor shown in the song from the movie doesn't look anything like her. The film is available on YouTube and one can see that the child actor credited for the role is Master Sridhar. My dear friend Rajagopal Prabhakar, scrubbed through the video to look for her and stumbled onto one little blink-and-you-miss-it apparition of hers in the movie. So, for the purpose of this book, I have considered *Thunaivan* as Sridevi's bona fide movie debut.

Thunaivan, literally meaning 'companion', is the story of a devout Muruga worshipper who undergoes crises that test his faith and how he held steadfast in his belief even then. Valayutham is an orphan boy brought up in a Muruga temple, but is thrown out of the place when he's accused by the temple trustee of stealing a ruby from the Lord's spear. By the time the ruby is found, Valayutham is long gone. By a quirk of fate, he ends up as a fruit vendor; and then by dint of honesty and sheer hard work, he amasses a certain amount of wealth. He also marries a woman after his own heart. But to his utter dismay his wife, Maragatham, turns out to be an atheist. He makes his peace with it but faith plays spoilsport as their firstborn has major health issues. In order to save her son's life, Maragatham embraces her husband's faith and prays to Lord Muruga to spare the child. As the couple nearly kill themselves praying Muruga appears as a little boy and blesses them, making the child better.

Sridevi makes her appearance as Lord Muruga at around

the two-hour mark in the movie. Wearing a dhoti and smeared with vibhuti all over, she looks resplendent as a mischievous little god. She was miles ahead of child artistes who were usually put on the frame to merely look cute and draw some sympathetic reactions from the audience. Don't get me wrong. Little Sridevi was cuteness personified but even as a toddler, she was completely at ease with the camera. She seemed like a person who already exuded professionalism as an actor. There are barely a few minutes of screen time for her, but she had that can't-take-your-eyes-off-the-screen look that captured everyone's attention.

When I mentioned this to producer and national award-winning writer Dr G. Dhananjayan, he responded with a twinkle in his eye: 'Yeah. She was like that. That's why I say she was God's child. Nobody could define her. It's very difficult to define her. She was born with a gift from God. But she did it organically. That's the reason why a lot of it just happened to her. So if you were to go and ask her to intellectualize it, she couldn't.'

Just with her first movie, Sridevi had arrived in the South Indian film scene. And there were people eager to help, every step of the way. It was the trio of Kannadasan, Kamaraj and Chinnappa Thevar that put her on the path to stardom. However, it was a future chief minister of a state and a reigning superstar who, in a manner of speaking, consolidated her position as a star.

∾

Most non-Tamilians know Jayalalithaa as a fiery politician and one of the chief ministers of Tamil Nadu. But what many don't know is that she, like most popular politicians from the state, was an illustrious actress and a veritable superstar.

The only time Bollywood audiences had seen her on-screen was in *Izzat* (1968), where she was paired with Dharmendra (besides her two-minute-long dance sequence in the Kishore Kumar starrer *Man-Mauji* six years before *Izzat* released). As far as we know, *Izzat* left a bitter aftertaste for her and she never returned to do another Hindi film.

Jayalalithaa's life and career had many parallels with Sridevi's. Her mother Vedavalli dabbled in acting under the screen name, Sandhya. She too began working as a child, and that too with mythological roles. Her first role in Tamil cinema was in *Vennira Aadai* (1965), where she played a mentally ill woman whose partner dies in a car crash. Within months of this she joined forces with another legend, MGR, on *Aayirathil Oruvan*—the first in what was to become one of the most successful on-screen pairings in South Indian cinema. The Jayalalithaa–MGR alliance not only changed the face of Tamil cinema, but of the political arena of the Indian subcontinent as well. Between 1965 and 1973, they appeared in 28 blockbusters together. Both of them went on to become chief ministers of Tamil Nadu.

Even outside her pairings with MGR, Jayalalithaa was a force to be reckoned with. She locked horns with Sivaji Ganesan in *Galatta Kalyanam* (1968) and *Engirundho Vandhaal* (1970), and with R. Muthuraman in *Suryagandhi* (1973). She had more than 120 films to her credit, and came to be known as *kavarchi kanni* (pretty young woman). As one of the most successful heroines of her time, she worked across languages—in Tamil, Telugu, Kannada, Hindi and even an English film.

✐

In 1935, a young American man on his trip to India was offered a film to direct. Ellis R. Dungan had recently graduated in filmmaking from the University of Southern California. He was visiting his friend, Manik Lal Tandon, who was directing a Tamil film in Calcutta. Tandon was asked to direct another film called *Sathi Leelavathi*, but he just didn't have the bandwidth to commit to it. He asked his friend Ellis to take it up. Ellis Dungan plunged into making *Sathi Leelavathi* (1936). For a crucial negative role, he cast a young actor who was doing plays for a drama troupe. All of 19 years and unspeakably destitute, the boy couldn't believe the amount he was offered as advance. He showed the 100-rupee note to his brother and asked if it was even real money. This boy was none other than Maruthur Gopalan Ramachandran, sometimes known as Ramachander or MGR.

Ellis Dungan went on to make a name for himself as a director of Tamil and Telugu films, languages he didn't understand at all. Over the years that followed, Ramachandran became MGR—the hero of the masses. He chose his roles carefully, almost always playing the rebellious folk hero who fought on behalf of the working classes. As a school dropout, he came to be known as *vaathiyaar* (a teacher to the working classes). His songs became clarion calls for the people to wake up and break their shackles: 'Thoongathe, Thambi, Thoogathe (Do not sleep, brother, do not sleep).' Most of his films had dialogues espousing the glory of the Tamil people and how the oppressor needed to be taught a lesson. These rousing dialogues were often written by his future political bête noire, Muthuvel Karunanidhi, and had an incredible impact on the audience.

MGR had a 42-year-long career as a leading man, which is possibly the longest such stint in India. Even Dev Anand had stopped playing the true-blue leading man by that stage in his career. The word 'legend' falls criminally short of describing what MGR symbolizes in Tamil Nadu. Much like Rajinikanth later on, he was the hero of the multitudes and the *makkal thilagam* (king of the people). In contrast to his contemporary, the thespian Sivaji Ganesan, MGR's roles were magnified and considerably larger than life.

✍

In most of the iconic films that MGR starred in, there was one heroine rubbing shoulders with him: Jayalalithaa. The Jayalalithaa–MGR team went on a rampage through Tamil cinema of the 1960s and 1970s. It was during the height of their popularity that the little heroine of our story got to work with them. Sridevi co-starred with MGR and Jayalalithaa in *Nam Naadu* (quite literally translated for the title of the Rajesh Khanna-starrer it inspired: *Apna Desh*).

In 1969, MGR wanted to test the waters before taking the plunge into active politics. *Nam Naadu* was his attempt to gauge how people would respond to his political career. After the massively successful *Enga Veettu Pillai* (1965), a predecessor to *Ram aur Shyam* (1967), MGR got in touch with the producer (B. Nagi Reddy) urging him to make a film that will feature him as a leader of the people. The Telugu blockbuster *Kathanayakudu* (1969) seemed to be a perfect fit for this. They decided to remake it in Tamil as *Nam Naadu.*

Nam Naadu's hero, Durai (an overtly obvious nod to C.N. Annadurai, Tamil Nadu's first chief minister and one of MGR's political gurus), is an honest government official—an upright man who obstinately stands by the path of righteousness, come what may. His naive brother, Muthaiya, works for one of three powerful politicians in the neighbourhood. These politicians often run afoul of Durai for their illegal and corrupt means. This leads to a rift among the brothers and Durai starts living in the slums. He is supported by Alamelu (played by Jayalalithaa), a fiery girl who sells coconuts for a living.

Durai often spends time with his brother's children, a little boy called Raja and a girl named Selvi. The role of Selvi was played by Kutty Padmini, a prominent child actor during those times. The boy was played by Sridevi.

While talking to *IndiaGlitz*'s YouTube channel after Sridevi's passing, Kutty Padmini reminisced about their days shooting for *Nam Naadu*:

> While we were shooting for Nam Naadu, I had already acted in many other movies, so I was a little more experienced and slightly older than Sridevi. Sridevi was such a little child that she did not even know that she is a girl that's dressed up as a boy. Sridevi did not even realize that she was acting. She just did what she's being asked to do, like a parrot. I used to teach her a lot about where to look when the camera is placed a certain way. She used to listen to me. She was a very obedient child.[5]

Many have alluded to this quality of effortlessness in her. Even as a child, she seemed to be utterly at ease in front of the camera. It is natural for a kid to be slightly awkward when asked to behave a certain way when they are on camera. This is incredibly evident even in today's digital age when kids are practically exposed to the camera since their birth. But even in an era when cameras weren't all that ubiquitous,

---

[5]'Sridevi's Childhood Friend Kutty Padmini Interview | Tamil Actress Death 2018', YouTube, https://tinyurl.com/3ddxncs4. Accessed on 24 May 2023.

little Sridevi was completely at ease with the lens.

Unlike the information given in some recent books, Sridevi's role in *Nam Naadu* wasn't restricted to just the song 'Nalla Perai'. The children always appear together, on five different occasions, throughout the film. When Durai is thrown out of his brother's house, he feels a tug on his leg. Raja (played by Sridevi) is pulling at him, eyes welling up. Then when he is living on his own in the slums, the kids come to visit him leading to a touching reunion.

We don't have melancholy in movies anymore. I don't mean nobody sobs on screen. Today's audiences are uncomfortable with two things: silences and sorrow. If the actors don't speak for an extended period and there's no music, the audience shuffles in their seat. Even the worst setback in the characters' lives has to be sugar-coated these days. Sadness and melancholy, unless you are watching a Vishal Bharadwaj or an Anurag Kashyap movie, are not emotions anyone likes to explore in cinema anymore. Till the 1970s however, it was the other extreme. Deprivation, pain, separation and misery were essential in every film (unless it was an out-and-out comedy). Sad songs were a staple and every character playing a mother, sister or grandmother had to know how to weep on the screen. And sitting in the audience, you'd hear a sniff or two around you.

Sridevi, as a child, played this part phenomenally well. With her cherubic little face, the puffing of her lips and looking like she was about to burst into tears, she could melt the coldest of hearts. There are various such moments in *Nam Naadu* as well. When she weeps, you want to reach out and comfort her.

With this movie, her education had begun. As we will observe throughout the rest of this story, she was surrounded by stars and actors of great calibre and she absorbed everything like a sponge. Her formative years were spent in the company of these legends and through this uninhibited exposure, she was learning. She crossed paths with MGR and Jayalalithaa again. This was just the beginning.

Four

An Education

After *Nam Naadu*, Sridevi shared screen space a few more times with future chief ministers: MGR and Jayalalithaa. She did two more films with MGR and four with Jayalalithaa. The year following *Nam Naadu*, the three of them came together for *En Annan*.

A.J. Cronin, a Scottish novelist, was extremely popular among Indian filmmakers till the 1970s. His novels were known for their didactic content which suited the fabric of Indian cinema at the time, since most mainstream films those days aspired to tell stories with a moral core. *The Citadel* was a particularly favourite novel, with as many as three different films made based on it in three Indian languages: *Jiban Saikate* (in Bengali), *Tere Mere Sapne* (in Hindi) and *Madhura Swapnam* (in Telugu).

Another book of his that was perennially popular among our filmmakers was *Beyond this Place*, which was about a man discovering that his father was put behind bars for a crime he had nothing to do with. The man then proceeds to clear his father's name. *Beyond this Place* was made four times: *Sabar Uparey* (in Bengali, 1955), *Kala Pani* (Hindi, 1958), *Poola Rangadu* (Telugu, 1967) and *Jeet* (Hindi, 1972).

There was also *En Annan* (Tamil, 1970) which was an official remake of the aforementioned Telugu film.

MGR plays the lead role of Ranga in *En Annan*, flanked by Jayalalithaa as his paramour Vali Ammal. Vijaya Nirmala played his sister Thangam. Little Sridevi played the role of Thangam as a child. She appears during a brief flashback sequence where Ranga's father is framed and wrongfully imprisoned. And just like in *Nam Naadu*, her histrionics were on display here as well. She cries copiously, but here we also see the playful side of Sridevi come out (similar to her debut *Thunaivan*). In this scene, someone tries to explain to Ranga and Thangam how they have to live on their own. The kids take this in with a lot of cheer and Sridevi's face just lights up the screen.

This was Sridevi's second film with the superstars Jayalalithaa and MGR, though in this case she obviously didn't share screen space with them.

Alongside her acting career, Sridevi was a regular school-going kid but couldn't attend classes regularly. She was often spotted on the sets with a book. Between takes, she would study. However, if we know anything of Sridevi, her mind was probably obsessing over the next shot.

She later explained to Vir Sanghvi on a rare candid interview with *CNN News 18:* 'I remember as a child star I used to do two shifts. [...] My father was a lawyer and he was very keen that I should continue my studies. So we used to take a teacher along on locations. But after some time, it didn't help me. I was just too busy.'[6]

But her 'real education' was going on in full swing. Working multiple shifts in a day, she was constantly surrounded

[6]Sanghvi, Vir and Sameer Kumar Rai, 'Virtuosity: The Legendary Sridevi in Her Own Words', *News 18*, 25 February 2018, https://tinyurl.com/4eedwtt3. Accessed on 24 May 2023.

by the luminaries of South Indian cinema: Gemini Ganesan, Sivaji Ganesan, MGR, Savitri, Jayalalithaa, ANR, Krishna, B. Saroja Devi, Manorama and many others. Each one of them have legacies that an average Bollywood film lover may probably not be acquainted with. Most of the male actors mentioned above have later also played her on-screen lovers, especially the Telugu superstar Krishna.

Little Sridevi was playing around in the laps of legends, only mildly aware of their stature. This made acting with them, quite literally, child's play for her. She was watching them closely and learning. And along with these established legends, she was also crossing paths with future legends. For instance, her next project was with MGR, *Sange Muzhangu* (1972). The film was an official remake of *Jeevan Mrityu* (1970), which was itself inspired from the Bengali film *Jiban Mrityu* (1967). In this film, another young man was part of the crew. The 18-year-old boy was then an assistant to K. Thangappan, a popular choreographer those days. That boy was Kamal Haasan.

Just like Sridevi, Kamal Haasan had started acting at a young age. And if Sridevi's first film was backed by Chinnappa Thevar, Kamal was launched by another giant of Tamil cinema—A.V. Meiyappan (known as AVM). The famous AVM Studios in Chennai was named after him. Kamal faced the camera for the first time in a film called *Kalathur Kannamma* (1960), exactly nine years before Sridevi made her debut in *Thunaivan*. Kamal's performance was widely appreciated and he was awarded the President's Gold Medal for his work. He worked as a child artist for three more years, and then took a sabbatical to concentrate on his education. During this period, he worked in repertory theatre from time to time and also trained in various forms of classical dance. When he returned to cinema after a gap of seven years, his interest was not in acting but in choreography. He started his apprenticeship under Thangappan.

In *Sange Muzhangu* (1972), Sridevi played the younger version of MGR's sister. This character didn't exist in the Hindi or the Bengali versions and may have been created exclusively for that film. Sridevi didn't get to do a lot of song and dance in the film, so it is a matter of speculation as to whether she and Kamal ever crossed paths during the shoot. Nevertheless, the serendipity was interesting and within just four years of this they became a popular romantic pair in films. This started with *Kuttavum Shikshayum* (1976), a Malayalam film. During the shoot of *Sange Muzhangu*, Sridevi was nine and Kamal was 18.

Sridevi continued to work with Jayalalithaa in films like *Aathi Parasakthi*, where she played Lord Muruga once again; and in *Thirumangalyam* (noted for being Jayalalithaa's hundredth film). *Aathi Parasakthi* also starred Gemini Ganesan. MGR and Gemini Ganesan were two of the three popular pillars of Tamil cinema back in the day. Sridevi had, by then, started working regularly with the third pillar—Sivaji Ganesan—as well.

Sivaji Ganesan was hailed as the original thespian of Tamil cinema. While MGR appealed to the masses with his rousing songs, fight scenes and dialogues; Sivaji was known for his theatrics and intense performances. He played a variety of characters and his monologues were the stuff of legends. Born as Villupuram Chinnasamy Ganesan, his rechristening as Sivaji happened on the stage. He had worked for a succession of drama troupes—travelling and staging plays. Theatre was his learning ground. C.N. Annadurai had written a play called *Sivaji Kanda Indhu Rajyam*, for which MGR was supposed to play the role of Chhatrapati

Shivaji Maharaj; but he turned it down and the part went to Ganesan. He performed the role with his signature flamboyance. In the audience for one such performance was activist and politician, E.V.R. Periyar. He was so impressed with Ganesan's performance that during his speech after the play, it was Periyar who called him 'Sivaji' and suggested that he should henceforth be known as Sivaji Ganesan. As we now know, the name stuck.

Sivaji's first film *Parasakthi* (1952) is notable for his extended monologue in a courthouse. The scene is considered a classic and helped demonstrate to the world that a new star was born—one who could speak clear, well-enunciated Tamil dialogues. The Dravidian Movement was gaining ground, and some of the architects of the movement—like C.N. Annadurai and M. Karunanidhi—were the creative force behind many of the films which contributed to Sivaji's success. With *Manohara* (1954), *Veerapandiya Kattabomman* (1959) and *Pasamalar* (1961), Sivaji consolidated his stardom. For playing the title role in *Veerapandiya Kattabomman*, Sivaji won the best actor award at the Afro–Asian Film Festival held in Cairo in 1960, making him the first Indian actor to be honoured at an international film festival. He excelled in playing characters from diverse backgrounds and genres: historical and mythological figures, cops, bandits, revolutionaries, saints and murderers. It all came to a head when he played nine unique characters in the film *Navarathri* (1964).

The first significant film Sivaji and Sridevi did together was *Babu* (1971), where Sivaji played the title role of a kind-hearted rickshaw-puller. When the car of a well-to-do family breaks down in the middle of the street, Babu carries them home on his rickshaw. He is touched by the egalitarian ideals of the family members and develops a bond with the little daughter, Ammu (played by Sridevi). Due to an unfortunate turn of events, Babu lands up in jail for a few years. When he is released, he realizes that Ammu's family had fallen on hard times and the little girl had no resort but to beg on the streets for alms. Babu then takes it upon himself to work hard and support the family financially and to ensure that Ammu gets the best education possible. But a grown-up and educated Ammu starts resenting the apparently uncouth Babu only to realize the error of her ways in the climax.

Sridevi had a lot of legroom to play little Ammu. Unlike the other films she was doing at this time, she wasn't just the hero's sister's childhood version. Ammu was cute, verbose and had ample screen time with the film's hero. There was plenty to chew on here, and she made full use of this opportunity. Sivaji was not the only big star in the film. Vijaysri, who played Babu's lover Kannamma, was known as the Marilyn Monroe of Tamil cinema. And then there was Sowcar Janaki, who played the role of Ammu's mother in the movie. An incredibly prolific heroine, Sowcar Janaki was incidentally known for her pairings with Sivaji Ganesan (though here she wasn't exactly a love interest).

Amidst this bevy of stars, Sridevi managed to make an impression. Nobody who had seen *Babu*, a blockbuster back in the day, could avoid being impacted by her portrayal of Ammu. As a blogger wrote later, 'Sridevi was a scene stealer in a film studded with superstars Sivaji Ganesan and Vijayasri.'[7]

Sridevi's 'schooling' wasn't restricted to actors alone. She was working with some of the best directors in the business. *Babu* was directed by A.C. Tirulokchandar, one

---

[7]'Sridevi as a Child Artist in Babu (1971)', *The Biggest Sridevi Fan Page*, 18 May 2020, https://tinyurl.com/yec85458. Accessed on 24 May 2023.

of AVM banner's most successful directors. According to a correspondent of *The New Indian Express*, 'The pairing of Tirulokchandar and Sivaji Ganesan was much like the Martin Scorsese–Robert De Niro combination, with the duo collaborating on 25 films.'[8] He was among those Tamil filmmakers who had also made successful Hindi films, most of which were remakes of Tamil movies, including the Dharmendra and Meena Kumari starrer *Main Bhi Ladki Hoon* (1964). He remade *Babu* in 1985 with Rajesh Khanna stepping into the shoes of Sivaji Ganesan. The little girl in this remake was played by Baby Geeta. A.C. Tirulokchandar also went on to direct Sridevi in many films later on.

Another significant film of Sridevi's from this period was *Kanimuthu Paappa* (1972). The director of the film was S.P. Muthuraman, Tirulokchandar's protégé who was debuting with this film. This was to prove the beginning of a long and prolific career filled with some remarkable films. Many of them starred young Rajinikanth, Kamal Haasan or Sridevi. They say he is the only filmmaker to have directed Rajinikanth in 25 films—the exact number of films his mentor is said to have made with Sivaji Ganesan. Parts of *Kanimuthu Paappa* seem to be inspired from Salim–Javed's debut script *Andaz* (1971), but it is a different film.

This movie is about two friends, Dr Ravi and Raja, a biker (played by R. Muthuraman and Jaishankar respectively), and their distinctive experiences with matrimony and familial life. Dr Ravi's wife dies at childbirth and he despises his son, while Raja's wife turns out to be a hedonist who neglects her daughter Uma (played by Sridevi). Raja also ends up as a widower when his wife dies in a freak accident. But

---

[8]'The Deiva Magan of All Directors, He Shared Special Bond with Sivaji Ganesan', *The New Indian Express*, 16 June 2016, https://tinyurl.com/mj5kramb. Accessed on 19 June 2023.

unlike his friend, he loves his daughter to bits. Sridevi's chemistry with Jaishankar as her father is charming. The way she screams 'Manager!' as soon as she hears her father arrive, makes it hard to comprehend that she had begun acting just a couple of years ago. The song, 'Chitti Sollu Sollu', based on 'Hai Na, Bolo Bolo' from *Andaz* makes full use of Sridevi's histrionics.

All these people little Sridevi was spending time with and getting her true education from—Sivaji Ganesan, MGR, S.P. Muthuraman, Jaishankar, Jayalalithaa, Gemini Ganesan (who took such a liking to her that later when she landed up in Bollywood, he called up his daughter Rekha to take care of their 'girl from the South')—were not just talented actors, they were legends. Dr G. Dhananjayan told me in an interview:

> I think she was the only actor who grew up on the sets. She was living in the set. She just developed it all on her own. And a lot of people kept telling her do this, do that, and keep on improving. She acted with a lot of legendary actors...she acted with Sivaji Ganesan... She learned from Sivaji Ganesan actively. [...] You know, what happened is she acted with lot of legendary people. So, she knew how they performed. And she would immediately do it. The only difference is a lot of people would act outside, this girl would never act outside. [...] Switch-on, and she will act... switch-off and she doesn't know what to do... She just doesn't know what to do. That's the reason why, when asked about it she didn't know how to explain the whole process. She couldn't explain the process at all.

Five

Malayalam: First Steps

What I am about to say is difficult to express without stereotyping or generalizing, but let me try. The South Indian film industry primarily constitutes films made in four different languages: Tamil, Telugu, Kannada and Malayalam. Needless to say, all of these languages represent distinctive cultural identities. The respective film industries have certain distinguishing traits.

Telugu cinema has traditionally been known for its unabashed masala entertainers, gleefully celebrated by the masses. Characterized by larger-than-life stories, exaggerated performances and flashy costumes, Telugu films have often been successfully remade in Hindi. In fact, they have revived many a career in Bollywood. Some of Dilip Kumar's most popular films were Telugu remakes (*Ram Aur Shyam, Insaniyat, Dharam Adhikari*), and Salman Khan's as well (*Judwaa, Wanted, Jai Ho, Ready, Kick*). However, the one actor whose filmography is littered with such remakes is Jeetendra (talked about later in the book). In recent times, Telugu cinema has witnessed a move towards a different kind of cinema, evinced by the rise of stars like Vijay Devarakonda, Rashmika Mandanna and Adivi Shesh. The staggering success of the *Baahubali* franchise, originally in Telugu, has challenged the very idea of labelling non-Hindi films as 'regional'.

Malayalam cinema sits on the other side of the spectrum. Films from Kerala are known for their subtlety and realistic style of storytelling. By and large, the audience is cinema-literate and there have been instances where the most artistic, contemplative films have struck box-office gold. But these are relative comparisons. Both Telugu and Malayalam film industries have dramatic musicals, mythologicals, social dramas and action films. However, on an average, Telugu films are more animated.

Karnataka had a close affinity with theatre and that had an impact on its cinema as well. There was a leaning towards experimental cinema like the works of B.V. Karanth, Girish Kasaravalli, Girish Karnad and the like. Again, Kannada cinema is not a monolith and massy entertainers have also thrived over the years.

Tamil cinema has had a unique trajectory as well, with a heady mix of masala crowd-pleasers as well as intense dramas. On the one hand MGR was making audiences sing along with him and urging the Tamil youth to wake up from their slumber, while on the other hand Sivaji Ganesan was regaling cinema lovers with performances that would make them cry their heart out. After them it was Rajinikanth and Kamal Haasan who respectively became the icon of the masses and an actor for the middle class.

Sridevi remains one of the few actors who found stardom in almost all these South Indian industries (except Kannada in which she did a sum total of six films, one of which was significant but we'll get to that later). Telugu was her mother tongue and having grown up in Tamil Nadu, Tamil came naturally to her as well. Although Malayalam wasn't a language she was particularly fluent in, she tried her best to speak it with alacrity. So much so that many viewers from Kerala were firm in their belief that Sridevi was Malayali. In fact, her first Malayalam film was her second release after her debut in *Thunaivan*. *Kumara Sambhavam* (1969) hit the theatres on 26 December 1969, trailing *Thunaivan* by six months. She once again played the deity she had gloriously portrayed in her first film. Lord Muruga is referred to as Subramaniya in Kerala, and that is who Sridevi was playing in the Malayalam film. It was based on the eponymous epic Sanskrit poem by the poet Kalidasa. It dwells on the circumstances surrounding the birth of Subramaniya and his parents Shiva and Parvati.

Sridevi was once again surrounded by legends during the making of this film. Gemini Ganesan played the role of Shiva, her father in the film. At this point, his real-life daughter Bhanurekha Ganesan was about to make her foray into Hindi films with *Sawan Bhadon* (1970). In later years when Sridevi stepped into the jungle of Bollywood, Bhanurekha was one of her closest friends and confidantes. To her fans, this elusive woman is known as Rekha.

The role of Parvati was played by Padmini in *Kumara Sambhavam*. Padmini was one of Bollywood's most popular early imports from down south. She famously featured in Raj Kapoor's *Jis Desh Mein Ganga Behta Hai* (1960) and *Mera Naam Joker* (1970), along with a host of Hindi films from the 1950s to the early 1980s. But in Tamil cinema, she had a legendary status and was the highest paid female actor in her heyday.

Sridevi played the role of a deity with great abandon, unfettered by any inhibition whatsoever. Even today, more than 50 years later, as you watch her on YouTube doing her impish shenanigans as Subramaniya, you can't take your eyes off the child. *Kumara Sambhavam*, directed by P.

Subramaniam, won the best film award at the Kerala State Film Awards which had been recently instituted. After the success of the film, P. Subramaniam cast Sridevi again in his next film *Swapnangal* (1970). *Swapnangal* has glimpses of the Sridevi who was destined to make the nation sway to her beats. The film begins with a song, 'Akkuthikkuthaana Varambel', likely a form of nursery rhyme. Sridevi is shown in her schoolyard, singing away with her playmates. This was possibly her first proper 'dance sequence'. When she did this movie, she was seven years old. This can probably be dismissed as fan-speak but even then, she had a terrific aura as a dancer. It made you want to shake a leg yourself.

Sridevi's character, Rajamma, is a cheerful and pleasant child who never shies away from a bit of mischief. Her mother is an angel and her father is anything but. An unfortunate mishap takes away Rajamma's ability to see. In this role, Sridevi adheres to Indian cinema's time-honoured traditional way of portraying the visually challenged which includes fluttering her eyelids while looking at the heavens. However, she does it with so much panache that even the hackneyed act seems genuine enough to melt the toughest of hearts. Upon the demise of her mother, Rajamma's father brought home a stepmother for her. The stepmother, true to the depiction of stepmothers in Indian films, didn't take too kindly to the little girl and her cuteness. There's a scene where she gives little Rajamma an earful and the girl looks distressed. The expression Sridevi summons to her face for this scene proves that she was no more just a 'child star'. She was a bona fide actor. Actress Gitanjali takes over Sridevi's role to play the grown-up Rajamma and the film then charts a different course.

In 2012, right before the release of *English Vinglish*, she was asked by a journalist from *The Print* about her 'secret relationship' with the camera. Sridevi said, 'I think it has to do with the fact that I started acting when I was too young to even realise what it was. [...] I could mug up two-page dialogues in five minutes. That's why it was no problem for me to do Hindi, Malayalam and Kannada films when I didn't understand the language.'[9]

A closer inspection of her acting in films during her childhood points to something interesting. She was at an age when children's minds are wide open to the world, absorbing knowledge like a sponge. And there was no maths or English crammed into her brain. In addition to mugging up, she was also acquiring the skill set essential to the craft of acting (albeit subconsciously).

Soon after *Swapnangal*, Sridevi appeared in the film that consolidated her stardom in a language she didn't even know well. If *Swapnangal* was about a child losing her eyesight, *Poompatta* begins with her losing her mother. But while in *Swapnangal* Sridevi was just the 'child star', here the story focussed on the little girl. Sarada (Sridevi's character) shares a close bond with her mother and is distraught when she passes away, leaving her an orphan. She lands up in the care of Devaki, her mother's friend who soon turns out to be a great specimen of the 'evil stepmother' and torments Sarada at every opportunity. And the opportunities are plenty. Sarada is relegated to domestic labour, serving Devaki and tending to her children. Her only friend is Sumathy (played by Roja Ramani), one of the three children, but she dares not speak up against her mother. Finally, Sarada's benefactors appear on the horizon. A kind-hearted couple adopts her.

[9]Singh, Harneet, 'Sridevi, the Queen of Double Roles, Needed No Man to Support Her on Screen', *The Print*, 25 February 2018, https://tinyurl.com/36nz7a2e. Accessed on 24 May 2023.

Poompatta (Butterfly) was a children's film, a category almost non-existent now, based on a short story by the acclaimed Malayali writer Karur Neelakanta Pillai. Little Sridevi carried the film on her shoulders, and this was possibly her first lead role. From the very first scene, she grabs your attention and holds it. Scenes in this movie that portray dignity and sacrifice in the midst of poverty are similar to those seen in hundreds of other films. What sets this film apart is the unbelievable dexterity of Sridevi, who executed the most mundane acts with incredible flair. When the actor is but eight years old, it seems even more unbelievable. The few scenes mentioned below make Sridevi's dexterity clear:

> **Exhibit 1:** Sarada sat cross-legged, making morsels of rice and putting them into her mouth. It suddenly occurred to her that her mother hadn't eaten. She tiptoes into the kitchen and paws through the pots and pails, only to realize there's not much left for her mother to eat. She cautiously looks over her shoulder and puts some food from her plate into the pot for her mother. She fills her remaining dinner with water to make it look fuller.

Little Sridevi performs this act with spectacular charm and maturity, as if she had been doing this for years. Her eyes, as she peeks behind to see if her mother is watching, speak volumes.

> **Exhibit 2:** Sarada is walking through the grove, with a look of pain and helplessness on her face. She's in an open field now, moving through the vegetation until she reaches a clear spot—her mother's eternal resting place. It was as if a dam inside of her had broken. In

between sobs, she tells her mother what she's been going through. It seems as though she's lying on her mother's lap.

It has been said that as a child actor Sridevi was just following her director's instructions, often imitating their actions. And that's what makes scenes like the one described above perplexing. It's not glycerine, those tears are real. Those sobs are real. She's out of breath, overcome by emotions. That is real. Maybe it's the mysterious 'reservoir' that all actors tap into. She wasn't a 'child actor' anymore. The 'poompatta' had blossomed.

Another notable Malayalam film during this phase was *Aana Valarthiya Vanampadiyude Makan* (1971), a sequel to an earlier film called *Aana Valarthiya Vanampadi* (1959). P. Subramaniam, the director, was an important entity in Malayalam cinema and he owned a studio in Trivandrum called Merryland Studios. He had his own story department where most of his films were written. *Aana Valarthiya Vanampadiyude Makan* was a jungle tale. This was a popular category of films from the 1950s onwards. They were mostly variants of the Tarzan story, with a human child growing up in the jungles surrounded by animals. Watching a variety of animals (mostly borrowed from circuses) perform feats like standing on their hind legs, delivering messages or shaking their heads to love songs was amusing to audiences those days. Another reason for the popularity of these films was that they presented an opportunity for the customary action scene where the hero would fight a (fake) tiger, leopard or python, which thereby enhanced his aura.

Aana Valarthiya Vanampadiyude Makan was possibly Sridevi's first multilingual film. Some of her earlier films had been dubbed in multiple languages, but this was the first instance where the same film had different language versions that were shot simultaneously. The Tamil version was called *Yaanai Valartha Vaanampadi Magan*, while the Telugu one was *Adavi Veerulu*. Gemini Ganesan played the Tarzan-esque hero in the Tamil and Malayalam versions, and Kantha Rao reprised the role in Telugu. Sridevi played the heroine as a young girl. The film begins with Sridevi and Master Prabhakar (playing the younger self of the hero) prancing about the garden to a delightful ditty. She's an absolute relish in the movie and not one step is out of place.

Some film journalists and historians from Kerala I interacted with seemed to be of the opinion that Sridevi didn't have a significant body of work in Malayalam cinema. On the contrary, her Malayalam work is equally fascinating and significant as her work in other industries. She featured in eight films with the celebrated Malayali filmmaker I.V. Sasi, and joined forces with Kamal Haasan in a spate of Malayalam films during the mid-1970s.

Six

Telugu: Easing into the Blockbusters

S ridevi's first Telugu film was *Maa Nanna Nirdoshi* (1970), where she met two of her most frequent collaborators: Dasari Narayana Rao, who directed her in many films when she turned heroine; and Telugu superstar Krishna who was her co-star in many later films.

Before proceeding, a few things need to be said about Krishna here. He happens to be Sridevi's most frequent collaborator. They worked together in 35 films, a number much higher than any of her other co-stars in any film industry. It figures because Krishna was incredibly prolific—in a five-decade-long career, he featured in over 350 films. Today's audiences, even Bollywood audiences, may be familiar with the work of his son—Mahesh Babu—whose films (dubbed in Hindi as *Tapori Tiger*, *Jigar Kaleja* and *International Khiladi*) are routinely aired on television (TV) channels like Sony Max and Zee Cinema. At the peak of his career, Krishna had 18 releases in a single year (1972), which is something of a record second only to Bengal's Prosenjit Chatterjee who had 22 releases in 2004.

Superstar Krishna, as he is known to millions of Telugu

film lovers across the world, was a massive star throughout the 1960s, '70s, '80s and '90s. He was known not just for his blockbusters, which he churned out with amazing regularity, but also for the technological innovation in the films he produced. While he began in the early 1960s, Krishna came into his own with *Gudachari 116* (1966) where he played Secret Agent 116 or Agent Gopi. Made just four years after the first James Bond outing, *Dr No* (1962), *Gudachari 116* virtually started the trend of Bond-style spy movies in India. The film was a runaway success that made a star out of Krishna and inspired countless sequels and imitations in various languages. He had an interesting connection with Jeetendra, the Bollywood star. Krishna was indirectly responsible for two spikes in Jeetendra's career: Jeetendra's first major hit *Farz* (1967) was a remake of *Gudachari 116*; and the film that gave Jeetendra's career a new lease of life in the 1980s, *Himmatwala* (1983), was also a remake of Krishna's *Ooruki Monagadu* (1981).

The Krishna–Sridevi dynamic also has some interesting trivia. Professionally, he was 19 years her senior. Sridevi played his daughter in *Vidhi Vilasam* (1970), his sister in *Devudulanti Manishi* (1975) and later played his mother in *Samajaniki Saval* (1979). The two eventually became one of the most celebrated romantic pairs of Telugu films. There was a point when both had the same person handling their appointments, Venkanna Babu S.P. who was also a producer.

In a single year (1980), Krishna and Sridevi had three films which ran for 100 days or more in theatres. Dasari Narayana Rao, who was an assistant on the sets of *Maa Nanna Nirdoshi*, directed the two of them in at least two multi-starrer films. Out of the 17 Hindi films that Jeetendra and Sridevi did together, many were official remakes of Krishna–Sridevi movies (including *Himmatwala, Mawaali, Jaani Dost, Maqsad* and a few others). Krishna launched Padmalaya Studios in 1972, which eventually produced films like *Himmatwala*, *Mawaali* and *Justice Chaudhury*—all featuring Sridevi with Jeetendra. Now, let's return to the sets of *Maa Nanna Nirdoshi*. The 26-year-old Krishna had a huge solo hit in the form of *Gudachari 116*, but he was still featuring in multi-starrers with senior stars like NTR and ANR. *Maa Nanna Nirdoshi* was one of the solo hero films he was offered. His heroine was Vijaya Nirmala who was incredibly prolific, both as a filmmaker as well as an actor. She holds the Guinness World Record for the maximum films made by a woman director (44), a fact that is as incredible as it is sad. Vijaya Nirmala had also married Krishna just a year before the movie. They stayed married until her death in 2019.

The plot of *Maa Nanna Nirdoshi* is not conventional. While following plenty of tropes of masala moviemaking, the film tried something that has been attempted only a handful times in Indian cinema—placing children at the centre of plots with adult themes. Dr Krishna (played by you-know-who) wins the affection of Radha (Vijaya Nirmala) due to his appreciation for what is good and pure. But her father, Zamindar Raja Chinnarao Bahadur, does not want his daughter to marry a commoner. She, like any respectable heroine, leaves her father's house and gets married to the man of her dreams. Simultaneously, engineer Chakrapani (played by Chittoor Nagayya) is gravely ill and Dr Krishna has been treating him. But the villain (played by Nagabhushanam) laces his medicine with poison and the good doctor is arrested for the murder of Chakrapani. Krishna's son (Master Shashi) is raised single-handedly by Radha, but she tells him that his father lives in the US. Raja Chinnarao's son, Balaji Rao, who does live in the US, dies in an accident in Minnesota (probably the only time the US state finds mention in a 1970s movie) leaving his daughter Sudha (played by Sridevi) behind. Sudha is shipped away to her grieving grandfather. At her new school she strikes up a friendship with Radha's son (who Radha has named Chinnarao after her estranged father). Sudha does not know that this is her cousin. Chinnarao Jr finds out about his father and meets him in jail, resolving to free him. How the two kids clear Dr Krishna's name forms the rest of the story.

Halfway through the film, there's an extended song sequence where the kids are performing on stage. You see little Sridevi dancing again. But this time there's order in her movements or in the 'steps'. You can see a glimpse of what was to come in about a decade. Legend has it that assistant director, Dasari Narayana Rao taught them a step or two. But the pièce de résistance is the popular song 'Enthenthe Dooram' where the children are out and about. And the seven-year-old Sridevi again holds your attention and her charm is indescribable. It was as if she was possessed and not of this world. And when you are watching, it feels like she owns you.

Maa Nanna Nirdoshi was followed by two more back-to-back films of Sridevi's with Krishna. The first one was *Agni Pariksha*, which many consider a lost film as there seems to be no trace of a copy or any plot description available. The second, on the other hand, is a significant film for Sridevi who was gaining popularity among Telugu audiences as a child star; and for Krishna, who was consolidating his stardom as a bankable leading man. That film is *Vidhi Vilasam* (1970).

The director was Tapi Chanakya, who was riding the wave of a superhit Hindi film he had made just three years prior to this. You may have heard of it. It was called *Ram Aur Shyam*. It starred Dilip Kumar in a double role. What you may not have heard though is that the film was a remake of Tapi's own Telugu blockbuster, *Raamudu Bheemudu* (1964), featuring NTR in a double role. Tapi Chanakya was like the Manmohan Desai of Telugu cinema. Lost and found was his speciality.

Vidhi Vilasam had the same cast as *Maa Nanna Nirdoshi.* Krishna and Vijaya Nirmala played the lead pair, Nagabhushanam was the villain and Vijaya Lalitha was the 'vamp'. The film itself is like the *Inception* of lost-and-found movies. Nirmala (played by Vijaya Nirmala) is raised by a nurse after her father lost her at a fair (it's not lost and found till you have a fair). When her adoptive mother passes away, Nirmala is about to end it all when Krishna (played by, erm, Krishna) saves her and sweeps her off her feet. They get married and the inevitable happens. A baby is on the way, and as luck would have it both Nirmala and their neighbour are pregnant at the same time. Then, a calamity befalls the town in Krishna's absence. Krishna arrives to find his house razed to the ground, his mother dead and his wife missing. Mistaking the daughter of his dead neighbour as his own, he raises her and names her Jyoti (Sridevi). Nirmala, very much alive, struggles with rearing her son on her own. Krishna's adoptive daughter and biological son meet on various occasions and fight tooth and nail. And this is the first time in her short career that Sridevi meets her match, in Master Ramu (who plays Ramu, Nirmala's son).

Master Ramu, born Chukkala Veera Venkata Rambabu, had just started working. However, his most widely known work came two years after this movie in 1972. It was a film called *Papam Pasivadu*, where Master Ramu plays a boy stranded in the vast Thar desert left to fend for himself. He has a dog, named Tommy, for company. The film was hugely successful and Master Ramu's work was widely acclaimed. In *Vidhi Vilasam,* the kids are supposed to be at each other's throats all the time and it is sadistically enjoyable. So far Sridevi had only played cute, goody-two-shoes characters, but here her histrionics were given free rein. In her entry scene, she picks up a musket exactly double her size and scares the daylights out of her domestic help. When she fights with Ramu, their gesticulations are evenly matched. Master Ramu gets at her with all he has and Sridevi responds with an equal amount of spunk. When she finds her father coddling her rival on his lap, she lashes out at him like a little tigress—claiming her father all to herself.

In the following year, Sridevi worked with two more of her future heroes: ANR and NTR. Her first film with ANR was *Srimanthudu* (1971) but they only shared substantial screen space in *Bharya Biddalu,* where she played his little sister. With NTR she first featured in *Badi Panthulu* (1972), which is part of a genealogy of films containing diverse films like Japanese master Yasujiro Ozu's *Tokyo Story,* Hollywood classic *Make Way for Tomorrow* and Bollywood's *School Master.*

Badi Panthulu is about Raghava Rao (played by NTR), an idealistic teacher who is handed over the reins of a school with the unruliest mob of kids. He wins them over by doing what a teacher does best. And when the time comes, they prove it to the world that he taught them well. But it is his own children who become his biggest defeat. They set him and his wife (played by Anjali Devi) apart in their twilight years, each child picking one spouse to take care of. Sridevi plays NTR and Anjali Devi's grandchild. She is rather fond of her grandmother and doesn't spare any opportunity to mock those who try to pick on her. Much like *Vidhi Vilasam,* Sridevi gets an opportunity here to sink her teeth into something that is refreshingly different from the weepy melodramas for which she was often cast. Here she is remarkably effective as the impish little kid whose heart is in the right place. Incidentally, *Badi Panthulu* was the remake of a Kannada film called *School Master* (1958). It was also remade in Hindi with the same title in 1959. It was the first Hindi film to feature Sivaji Ganesan in a cameo (his only other Hindi film was *Dharti*). It is believed that the central plot of these films may have originated in *Make Way for Tomorrow* (1937), which was also the inspiration for Yasujiro Ozu's *Tokyo Story* (1953).

Just like in *Sange Muzhangu* (previously mentioned) Sridevi crossed paths with Kamal Haasan in *Srimanthudu* (1971), where he was a dance assistant to Thangappan. By this time, Sridevi seemed to be the preferred choice whenever a girl child needed to be on-screen for a substantial role or if someone was needed to engage in some good old song-and-dance routine. Almost every other Telugu film she starred in featured songs with her as the central attraction. *Srimanthudu* was one of them. The song 'Chitti Potti Bommalu' makes full use of a whole range of stock expressions that she had learnt to summon at will. It was an elaborate romp. One can only picture the teenage Kamal Haasan helping the young Sridevi with her moves.

This was also around the time when Sridevi encountered the man who would eventually catapult her to stardom, not just in Telugu films but also in the national arena—K. Raghavendra Rao.

Seven

'Mubarak Ho, Aap ki Beti Heroine Ban Gayi'

Kovelamudi Surya Prakash Rao, or K.S. Prakash Rao as he became known, was born in a village far away from films. 470 km away, to be specific. K.S. Prakash Rao hailed from Kolavennu, a village in the Krishna district of Andhra Pradesh. His first serious brush with cinema was in 1938 when he watched *Mala Pilla*, a film that showed a love story between a Dalit girl and a Brahmin boy. In a region (and country) riddled with caste conflicts since antiquity, the film created quite a stir. K.S. Prakash Rao wrote a review on this, and the director Gudavalli Ramabrahmam happened to read it. Ramabrahmam was mighty impressed with the clarity of thought in this lad, who was then, barely in his 20s. The veteran filmmaker wrote to the young film buff. One thing led to another and K.S. Prakash Rao found himself on the sets of Ramabrahmam's new film *Apavadu* (1941), playing a role in the film. K.S. Prakash assisted Ramabrahmam and other filmmakers like L.V. Prasad and soon, he started making his own films.

In the next four decades, he became one of Telugu cinema's most sought-after directors and the echoes of this success reached the shores of Bollywood. He directed Rajesh Khanna in the blockbuster *Prem Nagar* (1974), which was a remake of his own Telugu film *Prema Nagar* (1971). *Prema Nagar* was also remade in Tamil as *Vasantha Maligai*, starring Sivaji Ganesan. All three versions were directed by K.S. himself. K.S. became something of an icon in Telugu cinema, and among his many protégés were his nephew Kovelamudi Bapayya and his son Kovelamudi Raghavendra Rao. All three of them played a crucial role in Sridevi's story, Raghavendra Rao most of all. The trio made several iconic films with her in Telugu and, eventually, in Hindi. While she had her most productive and well-known collaborations with K. Raghavendra Rao, K. Bapayya helmed some of her landmark Bollywood films like *Mawaali* (1983), *Maqsad* (1984) and *Waqt Ki Awaz* (1988). K.S. Prakash Rao, besides directing some of Sridevi's childhood outings like *Naa Thammudu* and *Vasantha Maligai,* went on to wield the camera in several landmark Bollywood collaborations of hers with K. Raghavendra Rao, namely: *Himmatwala* (1983), *Jaani Dost* (1983), *Naya Kadam* (1984) and *Masterji* (1985).

K.S. Prakash Rao took Bapayya under his wing when his father died. His son K. Raghavendra Rao was also learning the ropes under him, assisting him on various movies like the one we are going to talk about now: *Naa Thammudu* (1971).

On a popular TV show called *Soundaryalahari*[10], K. Raghavendra Rao described how he and Sridevi's family shared a cordial relationship. They lived on the same street in Chennai and he used to visit them often. Her family used to solicit and factor in his advice about her career decisions. He was witness to her unrelenting work routine:

---

[10]'Soundaryalahari – సౌందర్యలహరి – 2nd November 2014', YouTube, https://tinyurl.com/39khprew. Accessed on 24 May 2023.

taking short naps in between shifts and being completely alert when the shot was ready again. He recalled one such day, when she was blissfully asleep and he picked her in his arms and took her to the shoot of *Naa Thammudu*. Her mother offered to come along, but he took full responsibility and assured her that he'll bring her back safe and sound. In a few hours, as we will see, he was going to regret this.

Naa Thammudu is the story of two brothers. The elder, a widower, endures all kind of sacrifices to make sure his brother Chandra (played by Sobhan Babu) becomes a doctor. But what makes all the pain seem bearable is the angelic presence of little Shanthi (played by Sridevi), Chandra's niece and the light of their lives. By this time, it is obvious that she was turning into something of a crowd-puller. The film could have done away with Shanthi's character, but it seems as though she was injected into the film to make use of Sridevi's histrionics. She was given ample screen space and plenty to do. There is a song sequence—of 5 minutes and 43 seconds—in which she briefly dresses up as Jawaharlal Nehru and pays tribute to the leader during Children's Day celebrations at her school. There's a point in the film where she tries to pull a fast one on her uncle by dressing up as a beggar. In another, she prances about in a sari. She does all of this with unbelievable charm.

About 75 per cent into the film, there was a scene where Sridevi had to run through the street to reach her uncle. The scene was shot at Mount Road, Chennai. The director, KS, held a white kerchief aflutter. He instructed her to run to the other side of the road as soon as he gave the signal. Even at that age, Sridevi was a director's actor. She followed instructions faithfully and precisely. KS signalled with the kerchief. Aiming for the other side, she sprinted as fast as she could across the busy street.

Shootings those days were not elaborate affairs as they are today. Safety measures were not such a big deal back then but the crew did try to ensure that the actors, especially children, were safe. They had scanned the road and K.S. Prakash waved only when they were sure it was clear. The whole thing happened within seconds. When she was halfway across the road, a speeding Ambassador car zoomed into the shot. Everyone gasped. At the speed of light, the black beast of a car shoved into the running child. Her tiny eight-year-old frame was tossed across by the impact. There was pandemonium. Crew members ran to her. She was knocked out cold.

Raghavendra Rao's heart sank. He had promised Rajeswari that he would bring Sridevi back home, safe and sound. He said that he pictured himself getting taken away by the cops. The unit converged on him. It was as if he had just committed a crime. A small crowd had started gathering around them. Raghavendra was sure that he would be beaten up, or worse. But mercifully, Sridevi came around. The car had brushed against her right leg. It was not a serious injury. Had she run just a second later or slower, the car would have run her over and a promising career would have been cut short rather tragically. But all was well. He heaved a sigh of relief. But he was reminded of what he had told her mother while leaving. All he could think of now was to get her home as swiftly as possible. Raghavendra picked the child up in his arms and didn't stop running till he reached Sridevi's house. He had a promise to keep.

Much like the now famous *Coolie* incident, this mishap found its way into the movie. The only distinction being that in this case, the scene is not highlighted. You have to look for it. And when you do, you are sure to gasp. I promise.

The next couple of years went by, with the young Sridevi

continuing to work with Krishna, NTR and ANR. She also appeared in *Bala Bharatam* (1972) which was about the childhood days of the Pandavas and Kauravas. She played the role of Gandhari's daughter and the Kauravas' only sister, Dusshala.

Akkineni Nageswara Rao worked with Sridevi in about 14 films, out of which four films had her as a child artist. From 1979 onwards, ANR and Sridevi were regularly paired as romantic leads. ANR was just a year younger to NTR and had a parallel career. ANR debuted as early as 1941 but his breakout role was Saratchandra Chattopadhyay's iconic moper, Devdas, in the Telugu/Tamil bilingual *Devadasu/Devadas* (1953). It was the third adaptation of the classic novel, after Naresh Mitra's silent version (1928) and P.C. Barua's trilingual version in Bengali, Hindi and Assamese (1935, 1936 and 1937 respectively). *Devadasu* is considered a high-water mark in the history of Telugu cinema and ANR was lauded for his dialogues which are still etched in public memory: '*Thaagithe maruva galanu, thaaganivvaru, marichipothe thaagagalanu, maruvanivvaru* (If I drink, I can forget, but they don't let me drink; if I forget, I can drink, but they don't let me forget).'

ANR didn't have the booming voice or imposing frame of NTR, but he more than made up for it with his own brand of histrionics. He was one of Telugu cinema's earliest bona fide dancing heroes. ANR went on to star in more than 250 films in leading roles, including some as a co-star with his colleague and competitor NTR. He even did a few with his own son, superstar Nagarjuna. *Anarkali, Mayabazar, Prema Nagar* and *Premabhishekam* are some of ANR's more popular films. The last two films were with Sridevi as his heroine. He went on to have a very productive collaboration with Sridevi.

Sridevi repeats her act from *Babu* in *Marapurani Manishi* (1973), this time with ANR playing the rickshaw-puller with the heart of gold, in place of Sivaji Ganesan. And the same year, all three of them—Sridevi, ANR and Sivaji Ganesan— came together for the Telugu biopic *Bhakta Tukaram*. In the movie, ANR played the title role, Sivaji portrayed Chhatrapati Shivaji Maharaj and Sridevi played Tukaram's daughter Kashibai.

Another remarkable Telugu work during this period is *Mallamma Katha* (1973), quite literally the story of Hemareddy Mallamma—a revered figure who was an ardent Shiva devotee from the Srisailam region of Andhra Pradesh. Sridevi played the childhood segments, while the grown-up Mallamma was played by Sarada. Sridevi had cooked up a bizarre cocktail of expressions, which she employed to great effect here: smile, flutter eyelids, puff up the cheeks, speak with an infantile affectation. She returned to this concoction of hers in *Moondram Pirai* (*Sadma* in Hindi) as well.

In 1975, we see her in *Yashoda Krishna* playing the eponymous god. There seems to be a jump here. A teenager now, she was a far cry from the child Muruga she played in so many films. In *Yashoda Krishna* she was given the role of the adolescent Krishna. She was growing up. Watching all these films is like watching her get older, and it is a delight. It is almost like a parent observing their child grow. The maturation was on both fronts—as she grew physically, her acting skills were also coming of age. After all, she had been working for more than six years without any significant breaks.

That same year, some films had her play 'grown-up' roles, like in *Devudulanti Manishi* (1975). She wasn't the heroine yet, but she was not playing the child either. On the sets of *Devudulanti Manishi* where Sridevi was playing an adolescent briefly romancing an actor (who at the time was known as a comedian), Krishna is known to have given her mother a piece of his mind. The apocryphal story goes that he advised her to not let Sridevi play these small-time roles since she was obviously capable of so much more.

And this is when 'it' happened. Three men paid Rajeswari and Sridevi a visit. They were director K.S. Rami Reddy; producer T.R. Subramanyam; and a cinematographer, who had then recently graduated from the Pune film institute, by the name of Balu Mahendra. Sridevi later said to Vir Sanghvi in an interview:

> They all came home and they told my mom if there's any sari, let her wear…we want to see. We didn't have any clue, we were just wondering what happened. They saw me in the sari and they just left. Next day I was shooting in the studio and the other people came and congratulated my mother. They said, 'Mubarak ho, aapki beti heroine ho gayi hai!' She was in shock. She was quite upset…she thought it was too early for me to become a heroine.[11]

This film was called *Anuragalu* (1975).

Three years before this, Bollywood producer and director Shakti Samanta introduced Bengali actress Moushumi Chatterjee in *Anuraag*. This was a film about a blind girl and her friendship with a child suffering from cancer (played by Master Satyajeet). *Anuragalu* was the official Telugu remake of this movie. Even the music by Chellapilla Satyam was heavily influenced by S.D. Burman's soundtrack for *Anuraag* (though Satyam added his own flourish). Sridevi repeated

---

[11]Sanghvi, Vir and Sameer Kumar Rai, 'Virtuosity: The Legendary Sridevi in Her Own Words', *News 18*, 25 February 2018, https://tinyurl.com/4eedwtt3. Accessed on 24 May 2023.

her blind-girl act from *Poompatta*, only this time she was wearing saris instead of frocks. But all the same, she tried to bring a sort of maturity to her mannerisms. There was no cutesy baby-talk anymore. She was a heroine and, by the looks of it, she understood this well. She was a tad awkward with the romantic bits, but she delivered the goods.

Her first romantic lead, her first hero, was Ravikanth. He portrayed the part played by Vinod Mehra in the original. He might also be the least well-known of all her heroes. There's little to no information about him online.

The almost sudden transition to a heroine didn't seem to unsettle her one bit. She had been playing little girls just months before and now she was, clad in saris, made to behave like a demure woman. Playtime was over. It was now time for her to take things to the next level.

Eight

Three's Company

Shivaji Rao Gaikwad, a Marathi kid from Bangalore, used to regale his friends with impressions of his namesake and idol Sivaji Ganesan. Shivaji Rao was a bus conductor, employed with the Bangalore Transport Service (BTS). The driver of his bus was a man called Raja Badhar who he still calls his friend, 50 years later. Biographer and author Naman Ramachandran has taken great pains to explain that he is not 'Raja Bahadur', as almost every media outlet prefers to call him. Shivaji Rao and Raja Badhar used to watch almost all the releases of Sivaji Ganesan and MGR, and Shivaji Rao would recreate Sivaji's scenes and mannerisms with uncanny precision. After work, the two of them would act in plays organized by the BTS Association. Young Shivaji Rao was consumed by his obsession with actors and acting, and this was not lost on his friends and family. With their encouragement, Shivaji Rao left Bangalore and headed for Chennai to be trained at the Madras Film Institute. This was around 1973, when Sridevi was getting her own training under the 'other Sivaji' and his colleagues MGR, Gemini Ganesan and Jayalalithaa—all giants of the Tamil film industry.

She worked again with Sivaji Ganesan on *Vasantha Maligai* (1972), directed by K.S. Prakash Rao. The year following that, she starred with Ganesan again in *Bharatha Vilas* (1973). She shared screen space with Jayalalithaa in *Aathi Parasakthi* (1971) and *Thirumangalyam* (1974). Sridevi plays a mute girl in the film, and her elder 'modern' sister was played by Lakshmi. From the 1970s till the '90s, 'modern' was used as a euphemism for promiscuous, especially to describe female characters. It was okay for a hero to be modern, even desirable. But a modern woman was viewed with scorn and derision. Interestingly, Lakshmi and Sridevi again played sisters one year later in the iconic Hindi superhit *Julie* (1975), directed by S.P. Muthuraman (who earlier made his debut with Sridevi in *Kanimuthu Paappa*). By this time, Sridevi had made a foray into the Hindi film industry with *Rani Mera Naam* (1972). Vijay Lalitha (mentioned earlier while talking of Sridevi's Telugu hits *Maa Nanna Nirdoshi* and *Vidhi Vilasam*) played the swashbuckling heroine who avenges her parents' deaths. Sridevi played the younger version of the heroine—the child who witnessed the killings.

During this period, Kamal Haasan was busy with his own journey. After his break from acting he started assisting dance master Thangappan, as he had previously done in Tamil films like *Sange Muzhangu* and Telugu films like *Srimanthudu*. When Master Thangappan himself took up the director's mantle for *Ammai Velankanni* (1971), Kamal Haasan not only assisted him in directing but also played a cameo as...Jesus Christ! After doing uncredited cameos in a number of films, it was Kailasam Balachander who gave him his first major break.

Kailasam Balachander, or KB Sir as the industry came to affectionately and respectfully call him, hailed from a small village in Tamil Nadu called Nallamangudi. His affair with storytelling began pretty early on when he and his friends used to stage plays at his house. As he advanced in years, Balachander started writing plays. During his university days at Annamalai, he staged and acted in many of them. This obsession carried on even during his employment at the Accountant General's office. He set up an amateur theatre group there as well. Soon, Balachander's playwriting skills were noticed and he started doing this professionally.

It was MGR who hired him to write dialogues for his film *Deiva Thai* (1964). Within a year, Balachander directed his first film, *Neerkumizhi*, adapted from a play written by him. He was incredibly prolific and the 1960s were a busy time for him, as not only did he keep making films and writing plays in Tamil but his stories were being made into films in Hindi as well (such as *Main Sunder Hoon* and *Oonche Log*). Between the 1970s and the 1990s, Indian cinema was populated by women characters who were either treated as sex objects or as walking-and-talking doormats. These characters would not just gleefully accept but also celebrate the 'sati-savitri' stereotype. In this era, there were only a handful of filmmakers who bucked this trend. Balachander was definitely one such director. His filmography is filled with women of blood, flesh and bones who were central to the narrative.

One such film was *Arangetram*, where the role of the protagonist was played by T.A. Prameela and Balachander offered the role of the brother to Kamal Haasan. The film is about a woman who took to sex work to put food on the table for her family. When they are made aware of her 'indignity', the whole family (including the brother she put through medical school), turn their backs on her. The very start of Kamal's career was through a grey character. But he was not the only one.

Having met K. Balachander at the film institute campus, Shivaji Rao told him very excitedly that he would like to work with the legend. But Shivaji Rao, at this time didn't know any Tamil. Besides Marathi, he was fluent in Kannada. Balachander, taken by the youngster's features and his general conduct, decided to give him a shot. But he had to learn Tamil, the language in which Balachander was making his film. Back home in Bangalore, Shivaji Rao incessantly practised speaking Tamil with his friend Raja Badhar (who was a native speaker). In 20 days time, when he met the director again, he had acquired conversational fluency in Tamil. Balachander was impressed. His faith in the boy wasn't unfounded. He signed him for *Apoorva Raagangal* (1975).

But the boy needed a new screen name as his namesake, Sivaji Ganesan, was the reigning superstar of Tamil filmdom. K. Balachander christened this new find of his after a character in *Oonche Log* (the Hindi version of his film, *Major Chandrakanth*). In *Oonche Log*, this role was played by Feroz Khan and was called Rajinikanth. Yes, Rajinikanth was named after a role which Feroz Khan played. In *Apoorva Raagangal*, Kamal Haasan played a young man falling helplessly in love with an older woman and Shivaji Rao, now known as Rajinikanth, played the woman's ex-husband.

While these two men were in their 20s, Sridevi was in her early teens and already quite prolific. Rajinikanth was just getting started and Kamal had done a few films as a child artist and was already a star. However, in terms of sheer prolificacy, Sridevi was a 'senior' to both of these legends. Balachander was launching his next film which was a remake of the Telugu film *O Seeta Katha* (1974), a unique revenge drama. For the lead, he was looking to launch a new heroine. It was during this time that Sridevi caught his attention. Rajinikanth was cast as the villain and Kamal Haasan played a cameo as her lover. But in many ways, Rajinikanth was cast opposite Sridevi. Like how Heath Ledger was once cast opposite Christian Bale. It was Sridevi's first 'adult' role in a Tamil film and this itself was going to be one of her career's most remarkable films.

In *Moondru Mudichu*, Selvi (Sridevi) is in a relationship with Balaji (Kamal Haasan) but his shady friend and roommate, Prasad (Rajinikanth), has a roving eye. Prasad always tries to act fresh with Selvi when Balaji is not around. Selvi tries to warn Balaji but he ignores her, since Prasad behaves normally in his presence. Prasad also sleeps around with other women, often taking advantage of their weakness. Selvi knows this but she's helpless as Balaji won't hear a word against his friend. Prasad takes advantage of this and tries to drive a wedge between the couple. When they decide to go for a boating trip on the lake, Balaji invites Prasad to demonstrate that the latter can be trusted. An opportunity presents itself and Prasad throws his friend off the boat. Selvi screams in terror and agony but Prasad doesn't move a muscle to save Balaji, who drowns. It's a double whammy as Selvi later finds out that her sister—the only earning member of the family—had suffered an accident which burnt her face so she couldn't act in the movies anymore (which was her source of income).

Selvi accepts a position as a governess in a mansion where an elderly widower (N. Vishwanathan or 'Calcutta' Vishwanathan) lives with his young children. When his eldest son comes to visit, she is shocked to discover that this son is Prasad. The son is equally shocked and tries to get close to her but the circumstances don't permit it. He challenges her by saying that eventually he will end up marrying her.

Unaware of their history, the widower decides to get Selvi married to Prasad. Burning with rage and an all-consuming desire to avenge her lover, Selvi convinces the elderly man to marry her instead. She not only becomes the lady of the house, but a stepmother to the man who went to extreme lengths to seduce her. She rubs this in every time they encounter each other, insisting that he call her mother. It is the ultimate revenge.

Now, try and picture this story. It's one of the most striking revenge stories out there. Sridevi gets an opportunity to sink her teeth into a role and she goes all in. All her life she had some of the best teachers that cinema could offer, but hitherto she was doing all the learning through observation. In Balachander she found a teacher who was eager to mould and shape her into a refined actress. And she was hungry. This resulted in a firework performance. Sridevi sparkled as Selvi in the role of a lifetime.

Renowned actor and playwright T. Krishnan, who came to be known as 'Kavithalayaa' Krishnan because of his long association with K. Balachander's Kavithalayaa Productions, said to me in an interview: '*Moondru Mudichu* was the film in which she was introduced as the heroine. It was an iconic film...it was a great film. Suddenly, out of the blue, she burst into the scene. We never thought of her as a heroine. We always thought of her as a little girl...'

When I remarked how strange it was for her to choose that role as her debut vehicle in Tamil, he added:

KB (K. Balachander) must have been a great influence. Mr KB was a legend and he had introduced Kamal Haasan and Rajinikanth. The 'star maker', so to speak. Nobody questions KB. At that point of time, I don't think she would have questioned KB. Nor was she in a position to question also. And her mom would have agreed... See, KB always was a maverick in casting. Always used to think out of the box... Always a little maverick... Little out of the box he used to think...

The helplessness in Selvi's eyes when Balaji refuses to pay heed to her is as palpable as the rage and hatred she harbours for Prasad. Rajinikanth also nails it as the evil man with no redemption in sight (watch the climax and you'll know what I'm talking about). Some of the scenes between Sridevi and Rajinikanth are incredible. She is the hero of the piece and he is the villain. And that doesn't even begin to describe what they share in the film.

In one scene, she brings one of the women Prasad had earlier wronged to the mansion. This woman has now given birth to his baby. Obviously, he is not amused with this development. After a confrontational song, Prasad is still fuming when Selvi comes looking for her 'son'. Then she nonchalantly asks him to come and have his breakfast. She says she'll get him married to the woman who had his child. Selvi had managed to beat his challenge, but the 'balance of wedding' was still pending. She wants to pay him back by arranging his marriage with that woman.

There's a lot to unpack in this movie. Sridevi was no longer a child artist, nor a teenager speaking to a man 13 years her senior. She was speaking to her tormentor who she had vanquished by turning into his 'mother'. She was rubbing it in by admonishing him as her wayward 'son'. Sridevi delivers all this and more, in her style. And here the 13-year-old girl reminds me of a young Shabana Azmi, or even an early Smita Patil.

When I mentioned all of this to ace movie critic Baradwaj Rangan, he was amused. He said:

I don't think she was a very natural actress if that's what you mean. When you name Shabana or Smita, I was a little surprised because that realistic school of acting was never hers. She was always from the Navarasa School of acting, where everything was a little exaggerated for commercial effect. And I mean this in a nice way because that's just a different style. So, I don't think she was realistic as an actress, but she could kind of be convincing about whatever emotion she wanted to play. And I think, you know, she had certain ticks that she did very well, like she would let her lower lip quiver and, you know, she would put water on herself to suggest sweat in a tense moment or something. Those are some things that she did. But overall, she was a very, very good commercial film actress and I say this as an opposite to...say a Smita Patil, who was not a very good commercial film actress. She kind of floundered in that zone. You know, she was very uncomfortable with it, like when you see her in that song from *Shakti*, 'Humne Sanam ko Khat Likha'. She's trying but something's not coming through, you know, and in this zone Sridevi knew her way around.

At this point in her career, Sridevi was a far cry from the child gods that she used to portray. She had blossomed into a goddess herself.

Nine

Red Roses at Sixteen

There are many clichéd turns of phrase in film journalism. There are many expressions like 'ushered in a new age', 'the end of an era' or the phrase 'changed the face of…'. But in some cases, these phrases ring truer than anything else. There was one film that truly changed the face of Tamil cinema in the 1970s. Tamil cinema never did have an 'art cinema movement' in that sense. Cinema in Tamil Nadu was always a medium of mass consumption and entertainment. But within this template, there have been experimentations galore. An early example of this would be *Andha Naal* (1954), which was a murder mystery without a single song in it. Balachander's body of work kept pushing the envelope of popular cinema, with plots that could hardly be classified as mere entertainment. And there was another filmmaker who, with his debut, hit the very foundations of what constituted commercial Tamil filmmaking in the 1970s.

This filmmaker was born in 1942 in Allinagaram—an approximately 32 km drive from Pannaipuram, Tamil Nadu (where maestro Ilaiyaraaja was born a year later). In his school days, his obsession with movies led him to recite whole dialogues from Sivaji Ganesan's iconic film *Parasakthi*.

His teacher reprimanded him for this initially, but after the class handed him a book of plays. He ended up staging a lot of plays at school. He often wrote and directed them. He also acted in them. He then went to Madras, the epicentre of all South Indian film industries in those days. He was looking for that one elusive break. It was the early 1960s and he was looking for work. One day while looking for a place to eat at the Pondybazar area of Madras, he saw posters of a Kannada film called *Belli Moda*. Despite having no understanding of the language (his mother tongue was Tamil), he went in to watch the film at Rajkumari Theatre. He used up all his lunch money to watch it. He was so moved by the realistic tone of the film that he decided to assist the director of the film, Puttanna Kanagal. He reached out to Ilaiyaraaja, who he knew previously. Through a musician in Ilaiyaraaja's troupe, he managed to get in touch with Puttanna Kanagal and assist him on his Tamil film *Irulum Oliyum* (1971). And that's the story of how Bharathiraja entered the world of cinema.

After assisting a few other directors, Bharathiraja set about to film the story he had nourished and nurtured in his head ever since he was in the ninth standard—the story of a girl called Mayil. The character was based on a woman from his town. Two things were clear in his mind: the movie would be the story of Mayil and that it would be shot in real locations. While shooting outdoors was not unheard of—whole swathes of *Moondru Mudichu* were shot outdoors—making a film in locations instead of studio sets was still very new in Tamil cinema. National Film Development Corporation (NFDC) of India was supposed to back the film, and it was supposed to be shot in real locations in black and white. However, NFDC backed out of the project at the last moment. Bharathiraja went ahead and made the film anyway. It was eventually produced by S.A. Rajkannu. He got his friend Ilaiyaraaja to compose the music for the film. The film was initially titled *Mayil*, after his heroine, but it was later changed to *Pathinaru Vayathinile* (which translates to 'at the age of sixteen').

∽

Around that time, Sridevi was doing adult roles in Malayalam films as well. After graduating to adult roles in Telugu and Tamil cinema, she also did two back-to-back Malayalam films with director I.V. Sasi: *Aalinganam* and *Abhinandanam* (both in 1976). In the latter film, she was still an adolescent but in *Aalinganam* she played the lead. The film is not an easy watch and nor is its remake *Pagalil Oru Iravu* (1979).

In the movie, Bindu (Sridevi) gives in to the charms of Vinod (Vincent) and they tie the knot. But there seems to be a problem. Bindu seems to have intimacy issues. The very idea of sex fills her with dread. Despite this, they consummate the marriage. Soon, she is carrying a baby but a sudden fall from the stairs results in a miscarriage. From this point on, she gets hallucinations and seems to be losing her mind. Bindu is diagnosed with 'retrograde hysteria'. When a relative of Vinod's (Raghavan) returns from the US, he gets the shock of his life seeing Bindu. Many years ago, when Bindu was much younger he had met her and forcibly impregnated her. Her mother had secretly taken her to a jaunt in the hills and got an abortion done. When Vinod finds out about this, he refuses to accept Bindu. Vinod assumes that she deliberately hid the whole story from him. Eventually Raghavan's character gets what is coming for him and all's well as Vinod 'accepts' his wife.

If the plot itself is a bit problematic, it's made even more troubling by the fact that there are plenty of intimate scenes featuring the then 13-year-old Sridevi. The song 'Nimishadhalangal' (a brilliant composition, by the way) seems disturbing when you know how old she was when the film was shot. She was playing a mature woman in all her other films as well, but these scenes in particular are difficult to watch...and not in a good way.

Nevertheless, when Bharathiraja cast her as Mayil in *Pathinaru Vayathinile* she slipped into the role without him having to spoon-feed her. She *became* Mayil.

In the movie, Mayil is not your average village schoolgirl—at least not like the ones you saw in the movies those days. She has ambitions. She wants to become a teacher and marry a city-bred man. Her mother shelters a bumpkin with physical deformities—a man named Gopalakrishnan (Kamal Haasan)—who the villagers don't even grant the dignity of being called by his real name. They all prefer to call him 'Chappani', a term referring to his deformity. Chappani secretly adores Mayil, but she's too starry-eyed to notice that. She is on her own trip, drunk on her dreams. She finds the man of her dreams in the village doctor, but he breaks her heart. It is when she loses her mother and Chappani stands by her unwaveringly that she realizes that he is the only man worthy of her love. Chappani is beside himself with joy. Egged on by her, he insists on being called by his real name—even smacking the village bully Parattaiyan (Rajinikanth) when he refuses to comply. It all comes to a head when Parattaiyan arrives seeking revenge.

The film brought Kamal Haasan, Rajinikanth and Sridevi together after *Moondru Mudichu*. Kamal was a massive star and Rajinikanth was getting a lot of attention for playing darkish characters with elan. Both of them did a phenomenal job with their performances. Kamal's turn as Chappani was stellar. It even earned him a 'degree' from his mentor, Balachander—which was Kamal's way of referring to appreciative letters he got from the maverick director. Rajinikanth also delivers the goods, playing a man who's evil to the hilt. But the one who captured the imagination of the crowds was Sridevi. She was Bharathiraja's dream girl. His Mayil. He later said in an interview:

> I convinced her that my character was not modern, but a rustic girl wearing langa voni. She said, 'Sir, because of your character, I am not wearing any makeup at all...can I do just a little?' I said, 'Okay, maybe just a little.' After the film's shooting got over, other actors left the set hurriedly, but Sridevi was in tears. When I asked her why she was crying, she said that I don't want to leave this place [set]. I haven't seen any other actor who's sentimental about the place of shooting. I felt deeply about this.[12]

Pathinaru Vayathinile swept all the awards and won a lot of acclaim for the director and his cast and crew. S. Janaki won a National Film Award for best female playback singer; Kamal Haasan and Sridevi won Filmfare Awards (South) for their performances; and Bharathiraja, Kamal Haasan and S. Janaki won the Tamil Nadu State Film Awards. It was not just the awards, the film won over the masses too. 'With M.G. Ramachandran and Sivaji Ganesan sharing all the Tamil fans between themselves, we were left with very little space and it almost choked us. In fact, it prompted us

---

[12]'My Dream Character Mayil: Bharathiraja about Sridevi's Involvement in 16 Vayathinile | Death Video', YouTube, https://tinyurl.com/2cmp92fx. Accessed on 29 May 2023.

to experiment creatively to get us noticed in the industry,' Bharathiraja later said in an interview.[13]

With the humongous success of the film, both in terms of the box-office and by way of critical acclaim, Bharathiraja came forth as one of the young Tamil filmmakers to watch out for. In fact, the mighty Balachander was so impressed that he said, 'I am his first fan and proud to be so.'[14] The film has inspired many Tamil filmmakers and actors of the current generation as well. *Thani Oruvan* and *Ponniyin Selvan* star Jayam Ravi said to *The Hindu*, 'When I watched 16 Vayathinile for the first time, I was flummoxed by the kind of film it was. I could not figure out if it was made for the film festival circuit or if it was a commercial movie. It was something new to Tamil cinema, and everything about it felt natural.'[15]

The 'Team Bharathiraja' also brought about a wave of talented technicians, craftsmen and filmmakers. One of them was K. Bhagyaraj, who went on to be a prolific filmmaker himself. *Pathinaru Vayathinile* was a feather on Sridevi's cap like no other. It not only brought her on the map as a serious actress, but also propelled her to stardom.

With *Moondru Mudichu* and *Pathinaru Vayathinile* the trio (of Sridevi, Kamal Haasan and Rajinikanth) came to the fore as bankable stars, albeit at different levels. For the next few years, there were around 50 films between the three of them. Around the early 1980s, their paths diverged but till then their paths kept crossing. Sridevi did 18 films with

[13]'Man behind the 1970s Wave', *Frontline*, 2 October 2013, https://tinyurl. com/msu99zk5. Accessed on 19 May 2023.

[14]Ramachandran, Naman, *Rajinikanth: The Definitive Biography*, Penguin, 12 December 2012, p. 68.

[15]Kumar, Pradeep, 'Why Jayam Ravi Considers "Bhuvana Oru Kelvi Kuri" an Important Film', *The Hindu*, 14 September 2019, https://tinyurl. com/2paeyk5c. Accessed on 19 May 2023.

Rajinikanth and 27 films with Kamal Haasan. Rajinikanth and Kamal Haasan starred together in 13 films, and all three of them featured together in three films. In my head, a vivid picture emerges of these three bantering on the sets. I asked veteran Tamil film journalist, film historian and producer/director Chitra Lakshmanan about their equation. He said:

Rajinikanth was a small-time actor at that time. *Moondru Mudichu* [MM] must be his seventh or eighth film, but for Sridevi, she had opportunities like MM, *Pathinaru Vayathinile* with Kamal Haasan. So, she has grown much faster. In *Pathinaru Vayathinile*, Rajinikanth was only playing second fiddle to Kamal because he was the bad guy, so Rajini came a little later but Kamal was already a star at that time. Rajinikanth first met Kamal in Kalakendra office. He was just picked up to act in a particular scene. It was his first day and Kamal Haasan walks in. Rajini greets him saying, 'I have seen you in *Sollathan Ninaikiren.* It was some extraordinary acting.' Right after *Arangetram*, he even did *Sollathan Ninaikiren* with Balachander. It had a powerful role for Kamal. He played a slightly villainous role. But that was the main role in the film. So he was already a star.

∽

Around this time, Sridevi appeared in two other movies that pushed the boundaries of popular cinema: *Gayathri* and *Kavikkuyil*. Both the films featured Rajinikanth.

Kavikkuyil is a love story set in a village. Rajinikanth plays Sridevi's brother. She loves Sivakumar, a devout worshipper of Lord Krishna and a talented flautist. As she gets pregnant and they prepare for marriage, Sivakumar loses his memory in an accident. Sridevi waits for him to return. Although not comparable to *Pathinaru Vayathinile*, *Kavikkuyil* had two things common with that film—a rustic backdrop and excellent music. There is a fascinating composition called 'Chinna Kannan Azhaikkiraan', sung by renowned Carnatic vocalist Shri M. Balamuralikrishna. The film didn't do well but Ilaiyaraaja's music became popular. This was the film that consolidated his status as a leading music director in Tamil cinema. It was another very mature performance by Sridevi. She uses her eyes to good effect. Observe her very first scene, in the village bazaar. She just owns it.

Gayathri was written by Sujatha, a prominent author and screenwriter who later also wrote Shankar's *Enthiran* (2010). Sujatha had created a crime-fighting duo called Ganesh–Vasanth, both of them lawyers. Ganesh was the hero and Vasanth his sidekick.

When Rajarathnam's (Rajinikanth) sister gets him married to Gayathri (Sridevi), the young bride senses that something is amiss. There's more than meets the eye. The family members behave in a lewd manner with each other. She also realizes she is under house arrest and cannot step out under any circumstances. One night she finds Rajarathnam and his 'family members' engaged in an interaction with a scantily clad woman which is completely inappropriate. It all takes a nasty turn when she discovers her husband's mentally ill first wife in the outhouse. When confronted, Rajarathnam denies everything. The family finds a way to dispose of the ex-wife. At this point, Gayathri has had enough. She hides a note in an old magazine, which ends up with Ganesh (Jaishankar). A little digging reveals that Rajarathnam is a producer of porn films—he lures unsuspecting women to marry him and shoots videos with a hidden camera in the bedroom. Ganesh sets about to rescue Gayathri from the clutches of the creep.

Both Rajinikanth and Sridevi deliver impeccable performances. The film follows the beats of a thriller and Sridevi perfectly expresses shock, dismay and mounting fear on every dangerous discovery. Rajinikanth as Rajarathnam is pure evil.

Her next major film was a thriller as well and here too a dangerous, psychotic man was at the heart of the proceedings. This time, the man was Kamal Haasan. When Bharathiraja followed up his spectacular debut in *Pathinaru Vayathinile* with *Kizhake Pogum Rail* (1978)—another hard-hitting rural drama which he later remade in Bollywood with Dharmendra and Sunny Deol as *Saveray Wali Gaadi* (1986)—he was labelled as a filmmaker who could only make films set in villages. To allay that notion, Bharathiraja conceived *Sigappu Rojakkal* (Red Roses) along with his protégé K. Bhagyaraj. Later, he said in an online interview, 'I did my second film with her, *Sigappu Rojakkal*. She said, "You don't have to tell me the story…I will come wherever you want me to come." *Sigappu Rojakkal* had been the film for which the story wasn't even told to her.'[16]

Kamal Haasan too, had an author-backed role in the movie so there was no reason to not lap it up. The plot is about deep-seated misogyny that manifests in violent ways. The film begins with a man toiling away at a flower bed. He kills a rat and buries it, planting a rosebush over it. Kamal Haasan is Dileep, a rich playboy who indulges in what seems like harmless flirtation with women he meets.

---

[16]'My Dream Character Mayil : Bharathiraja about Sridevi's Involvement in 16 Vayathinile | Death Video', YouTube, https://tinyurl.com/2cmp92fx. Accessed on 29 May 2023.

He takes them home, makes passionate love to them and then proceeds to kill them in cold blood. He does this day in and day out, and his exploits are recorded on video. His psychotic adoptive father watches these videos with pleasure. They bury the bodies in the garden and plant roses over the graves. Because of an episode in his childhood, Dileep hates women deeply and takes it out on his victims. But when he meets Sarada (Sridevi), his heart skips a beat. He finally falls for a woman without wanting to kill her. They settle down in holy matrimony, and that's when things get interesting. Sarada notices Dileep's favourite house cat merrily licking a spot of blood. Then she lands up in his secret chamber where what he does is laid out in explicit detail on the walls. Sarada is filled with dread, convinced that she may very well be the next victim.

Kamal Haasan is magnificent as the psychopath. Not a lot of leading men in the 1970s, or the '80s even, would be able to pull off a serial killer convincingly. *Sigappu Rojakkal* was remade in Hindi by Bharathiraja himself as *Red Rose* (1980), with Rajesh Khanna playing the killer and Poonam Dhillon reprising Sridevi's part.

By this time, Sridevi had almost reached her prime. *Almost.* She could play anyone, do any kind of roles. There was remarkable confidence in this teenager playing women double her age.

Ten

Hit Parade

As mentioned in the previous chapter, Bharathiraja used to direct the Hindi remakes of his films as well. *Red Rose* (1980), *Lovers* (1983) and *Saveray Wali Gaadi* (1986) were all remakes of his Tamil films. He also made the Hindi version of his calling card, *Pathinaru Vayathinile*. It was called *Solva Sawan* (1979) and it became Sridevi's Bollywood debut as a heroine. Kamal Haasan's role of Chappani was reimagined for North Indian audiences by Amol Palekar. Rajinikanth's role was played by a very young Kulbhushan Kharbanda. The film turned out to be a massive dud. One may very well put the blame on casting but it must not have been an easy job considering the difference in milieu, culture and the tone of the film. Just like that, Sridevi's first Hindi film as a heroine sank without a trace (quite literally, as a copy of the film is difficult to come by). It was shown on Doordarshan back in the early 1990s, but that's about it.

While the Hindi version didn't work, the Telugu version of the same film paved the way for the 'superstar' Sridevi that we know and adore today.

It is fascinating how a passion for movies manifests

differently in different people. There are some who end up turning into directors and some get into acting. I also know people who are extremely passionate about the medium but would never consider a career in the movies. Midde Rama Rao was crazy about films even as a child. The bug bit him so hard that he dropped out of college and built a 'touring theatre' in his village. After a decade of experience as a film exhibitor, he joined forces with his exhibitor brother-in-law to start producing films. To get their feet wet, they started dubbing Tamil hits into Telugu. Having tasted some success, they wanted the real deal. Midde Rama Rao and his partners were now ready to produce a film in Telugu. This was also when *Pathinaru Vayathinile* became a rage in Tamil Nadu. They decided to remake it in Telugu but the producer of the film, S.A. Rajkannu, was nowhere to be found. It was established later that he had taken refuge at a hospital to evade the tax authorities. The film had become a huge money-spinner for him. Midde and his compatriots met Rajkannu and Bharathiraja at the hospital and managed to buy the rights for a remake for ₹1.25 lakh[17]. They even had a name in mind for directing the Telugu remake.

K. Raghavendra Rao had come a long way from his early days of working as an assistant in his father K.S. Prakash's films. He was by then a successful film director in the Telugu film industry. His latest film *Adavi Ramudu* (1977), starring NTR, was a great success. It was one of highest grossing movies of the decade. As he was contemplating his next project, these new producers approached him. Midde Rama Rao was apprehensive. After all, Raghavendra Rao was

---

[17]Sri, 'Padaharella Vayasu-1978', *Telugu Cinema*, 21 January 2007, https://tinyurl.com/mshs4kev. Accessed on 29 May 2023.

a star director in his prime and they were just starting off. But Raghavendra Rao jumped at the opportunity. Superstar Sobhan Babu was initially considered for the role played by Kamal Haasan, but since it wasn't a glamorous part it went to the critically acclaimed actor Chandra Mohan. The villainous role of Rajinikanth was given to Mohan Babu. For the lead role, Jaya Prada was a strong contender since she had been in the latest hit (*Adavi Ramudu*). But they needed a teenager. K. Raghavendra Rao insisted on casting Sridevi, the little girl who almost died on his watch. He had seen from close quarters what she could do. Now it was time to show the world what they could achieve together.

For Sridevi, this was her second Telugu film as a heroine after *Anuragalu*. That film hadn't done well. By now she was more confident as a heroine and the source material had worked brilliantly with Tamil audiences. Additionally, this was an opportunity to work again with Raghavendra *Gaaru* (an honorific title in Telugu culture) but this time as a heroine.

Sridevi was every bit as good as she was in the original. K. Nageshwar wrote in *Firstpost* about his experience of watching the Telugu version, *Padaharella Vayasu*, for the first time when he was, like Sridevi, 'not yet 16':

> It was a joy for film lovers to see Sridevi's magnificent performance in two contrasting situations in the movie. First, as a young aspirational girl imagining her future in the comfortable companionship of her lover, who is relatively well placed compared to her rustic background. Then, when he ditches her and her life turns topsy-turvy, she has to portray the character of someone reconciling to the reality of living with a physically challenged person. Sridevi performed

these strikingly different roles with unparalleled acting acumen and demonstrated a maturity quite unusual for her age. I was also not yet 16, and it took me a few years to fully appreciate the maturity in her portrayal, where I had previously simply delighted in it.[18]

Padaharella Vayasu became a massively successful film and it was loved almost as highly as its predecessor. Ram Gopal Varma (RGV) mentioned on the Telugu talk show *Soundaryalahari* that he watched the film 10 times when he was studying engineering. On the same show, director K. Raghavendra Rao explained how he made certain creative choices that made the film somewhat different from the original.[19]

In the Tamil original, Mayil (Sridevi) is seen standing on the railway platform as the cops take Gopal/Chappani (Kamal Haasan) away. She stands there long after the train has left and silently promises him that when he will be back, she will marry him. That's where the film ends. In *Padaharella Vayasu*, Malli (Sridevi) returns to the platform to look for Gopal (Chandra Mohan) but he isn't there. Crestfallen, she turns back towards the village holding the sacred thread that Gopal was to tie on her. Just as she is leaving she hears someone calling out to her and sure enough, it is Gopal. He ties the thread and they get married. That's the ending in the Telugu version.

Raghavendra Rao explains:

When a superhit Tamil movie comes to you for a remake, there are a lot of things to consider. In the

---

[18]Nageshwar, K., 'Sridevi's Hindi, Tamil Films Have Been Focus of Pundits, but It's Her Telugu Roles That Reflect Unparalleled Journey', *Firstpost*, 28 February 2018, https://tinyurl.com/bsfr394h. Accessed on 8 June 2023.

[19]'Soundaryalahari – సౌందర్యలహరి – 2nd November 2014', YouTube, https://tinyurl.com/y864ms2v. Accessed on 29 May 2023.

beginning of the film, she is waiting at the railway station. The rest of the movie is a flashback and in the end, we are back on the platform again with her. She waits for him; she believes that he would come. I thought why should we leave the girl waiting? So, we changed it a bit. Both Rajinikanth and Kamal Haasan called me, they said, 'Sir, please don't change the climax, let it be as it is, there may be an issue.' I think this is a nice story and when people watch, they think this could be our life.[20]

RGV, sitting on the couch for the show, agreed and said this ending was more fulfilling. K. Raghavendra Rao also employed another visual trick to accentuate the emotions in that final scene. He says, 'At that time there were these new filters for the camera, with different colours. Prakash (the cinematographer) was afraid to use the filters. We convinced him that it should look a little imaginary.' RGV nodded and said, 'That is cinema. Cinema is that.'[21]

Around three years and three months after the show was telecast, the world woke up to the horrible news of Sridevi's passing. RGV was distraught and wrote the following in his tribute to her on his Facebook page:

Back in the times when I was in engineering college in Vijayawada, I happened to see her first Telugu film *Padaharella Vayasu*. I was awestruck with her beauty and I walked out of the theatre in a daze thinking that she cannot be a real person and she has to be some fantasy form who somehow has taken a human shape. Then I saw her various other films, all of which constantly

---

[20]Ibid.
[21]Ibid.

created a higher bench mark of both her talent and her beauty. To me she looked like some being who has come from some other world in the outer space as a favour to bless us for a little while for all the good we might have done in this world.[22]

Like its Tamil counterpart, *Padaharella Vayasu* was a runaway hit at the box-office. It ran for more than 100 days in most centres. According to Midde Rama Rao, the producer, the film earned them a 'table profit of six lakhs', which was a princely sum in those days.[23]

∽

Sridevi was now a superstar in Telugu cinema, but she was still in her teens. In Tamil films, more often than not, she was working with Kamal Haasan and Rajinikanth. However, in Telugu cinema most of the actors who played her uncles and fathers were still in circulation as leading men and were to be her heroes. On the flip side, most of these actors were then on the better side of 40, still younger than the Khans in Bollywood today.

The next significant film for Sridevi was *Karthika Deepam* (1979). The film hit the jackpot and became a phenomenal success at the box-office. Her co-star in the film was Sobhan Babu, who had played her *chinnanna* (uncle) in *Naa Thammudu* just eight years before.

But one of Sridevi's most popular on-screen pairing was initiated with *Vetagadu* (1979), her second film with K.

[22]'Ram Gopal Varma's Love letter to Sridevi', *India Forums*, https://tinyurl.com/y965z87d. Accessed on 19 June 2023.
[23]'Interview with Midde Rama Rao... Interesting', *SBDBForums*, https://tinyurl.com/nsxs6scv. Accessed on 12 June 2023.

Raghavendra Rao as director. This pairing was with NTR, 30 years her senior. Since the superstar had played her grandfather just seven years ago in *Badi Panthulu*, nobody was convinced that this young girl should be cast opposite him on the screen. But it was director K. Raghavendra Rao who persuaded everyone. The result was a major blockbuster of the 1970s, which placed Sridevi in the first row of bankable female superstars in Telugu cinema back in the day.

In the TV show *Soundaryalahari*, Raghavendra Rao told RGV the story behind casting her in *Vetagadu*. He said:

Ramu, you can imagine how complicated it gets if producers go against you. Everyone was asking me, who would tell Rama Rao Sir [NTR]? What would people think if you cast a girl who acted as a grand-daughter opposite Rama Rao Gaaru? It won't work. But he liked me a lot. I said 'let me try once' and went to the sets to meet him. When he asked the purpose of my visit, I said, 'I will tell you after the shot,' but he insisted, saying, 'No problem...please go ahead and tell me.'

I said, 'Nothing Sir, just wanted to discuss about the heroine for our next film'. He said, 'What have you decided?'

I said, 'I am considering Sridevi.' He replied, 'Okay, so what's the problem?'

I said, 'She is 14, and everyone is worried about it.' He replied, 'So what, I am also 14!'

With *Padaharella Vayasu* Sridevi became famous. It was a silver jubilee and she was established as a glamorous actress. That glamour now had to be taken to stardom. To give her that stardom, we had to cast her opposite the Superstar: NTR. My intention was to get Sridevi on track. I had to change the original heroine of *Vetagadu*, and put someone more glamorous who could do several different get-ups. So I thought she is my best option. Then I shot a song first and got it edited to showcase to the producers, in order to gain their confidence.[24]

That song was 'Aaku Chaatu Pinde Tadise', in all probability Sridevi's first 'rain song'. The song has eerie similarities with that illustrious number from the 1997 Salman Khan hit *Judwaa*—'Tu Mere Dil Mein Bas Jaa'.

Sridevi, in the same show, adds to Raghavendra Rao's point: 'At the age of 14, I didn't feel like 14. The whole credit goes to Raghavendra Rao Gaaru. I mean I remember that he would do get-up, hairstyles and everything with full responsibility and interest. Each and every get-up in that movie was selected by him.'[25]

RGV also told a story of how *Vetagadu* inspired a song in one of his own films starring Sridevi and Nagarjuna, *Govinda Govinda* (1993). When RGV was watching the NTR–Sridevi movie in the theatre, the song 'Aaku Chaatu Pinde Tadise' had just played and there was a 10-second delay in changing the reels (if you're reading this book, I probably won't have to explain that these were pre-digital days and every film had a certain number of 'reels'), during which there was total silence in the theatre. And somebody screamed, 'I want to touch the feet of whoever gave birth to her!' and the whole theatre burst out clapping. RGV used this as fuel for the song 'Amma Bramha Devudo' in his film *Govinda Govinda*, where the hero is lauding Lord

[24]'Soundaryalahari – సందర్యలహరి – 2nd November 2014', YouTube, https:// tinyurl.com/y864ms2v. Accessed on 29 May 2023.
[25]Ibid.

Brahma for creating Sridevi's character.

Hits were coming thick and fast now. She was no longer just a child star. At this point Sridevi was already a bona fide star, a heroine who could pull in the crowds. There were whole films that rode on her dainty shoulders. Her journey to being a diva had began.

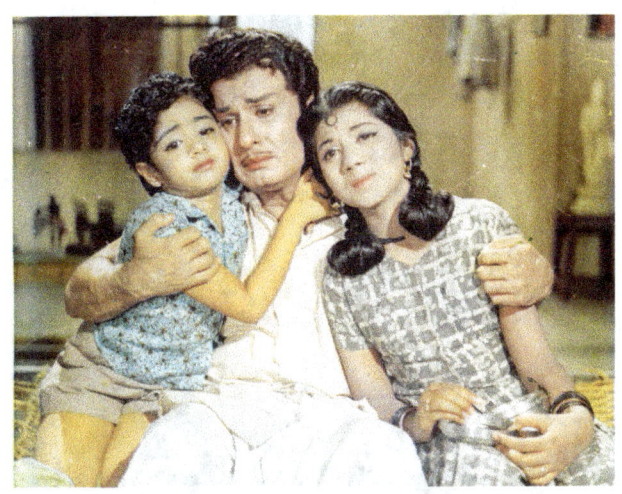

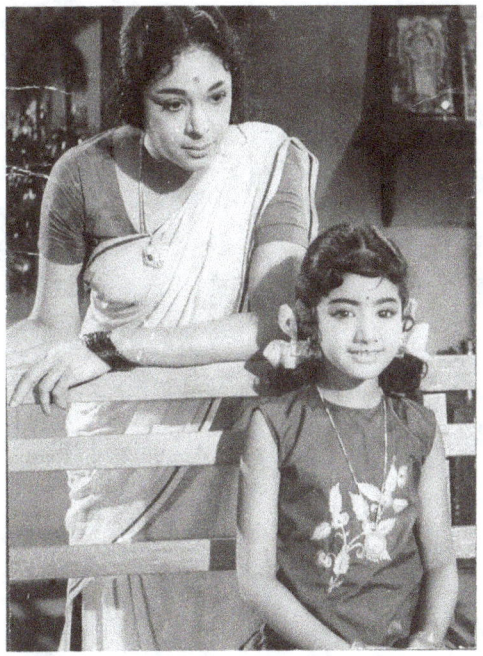

Top: Baby Sridevi (left), with the legendary M.G. Ramachandran in the 1969 political drama *Nam Naadu*, which also starred Jayalalithaa.

Bottom: A young Sridevi in *Poompatta* (1971), with noted character actress T.R. Omana essaying the role of the evil stepmother.

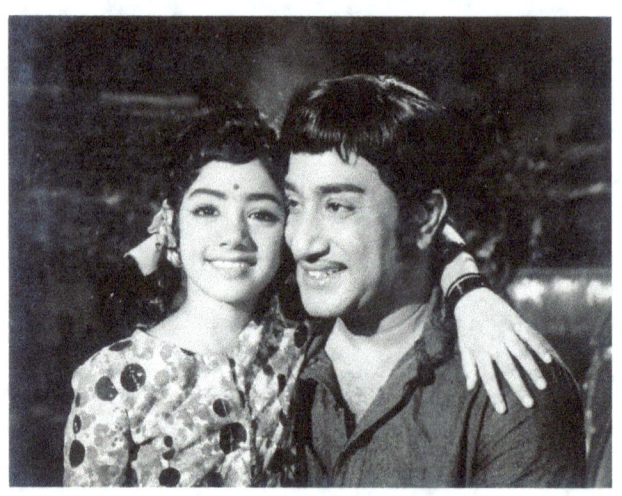

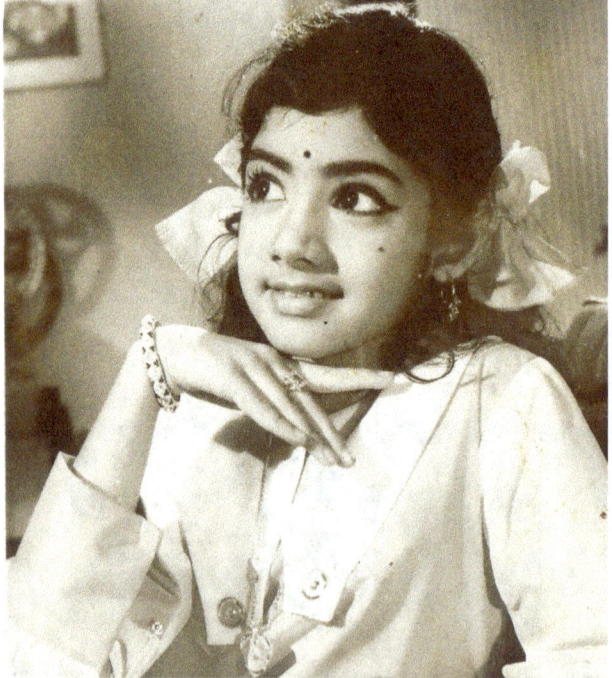

Top: Child-actor Sridevi with Sivaji Ganesan in the 1971 Tamil film *Babu.*

Bottom: Sridevi in the 1972 Tamil film, *Kanimuthu Paappa.*

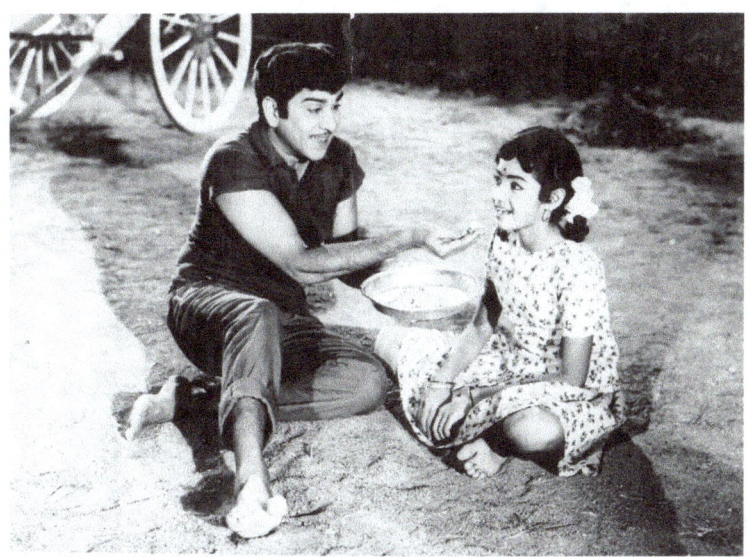

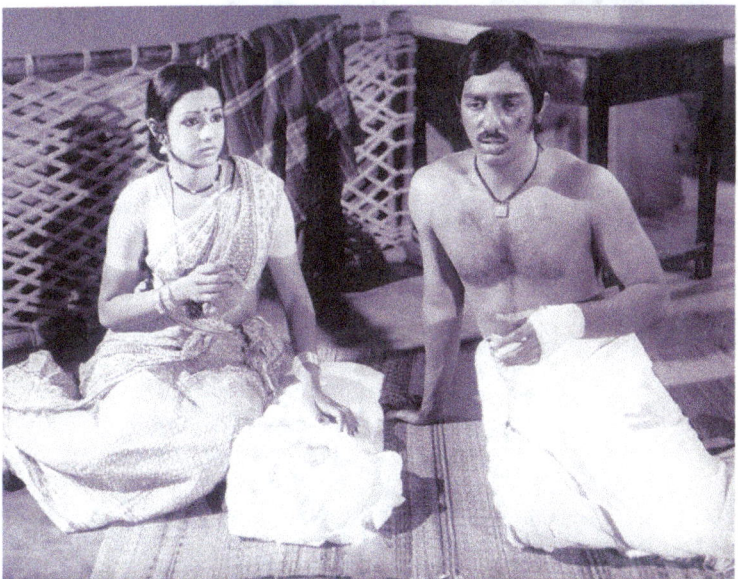

Top: A young Sridevi with Akkineni Nageswara Rao in the 1973 Telugu movie, *Marapurani Manishi*, directed by T. Rama Rao.

Bottom: A 14-year-old Sridevi with Kamal Haasan in *Pathinaru Vayathinile* (1977), which also starred Rajinikanth in a negative role.

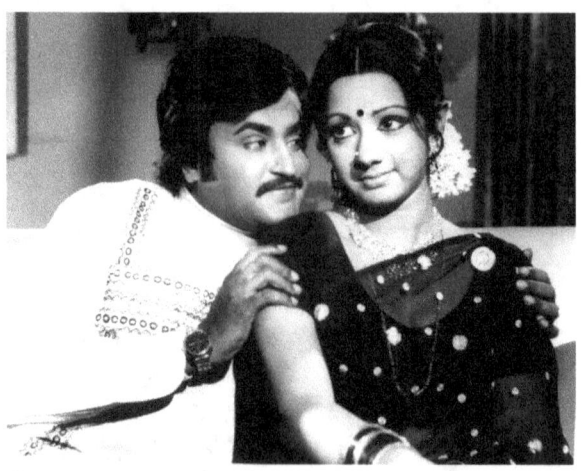

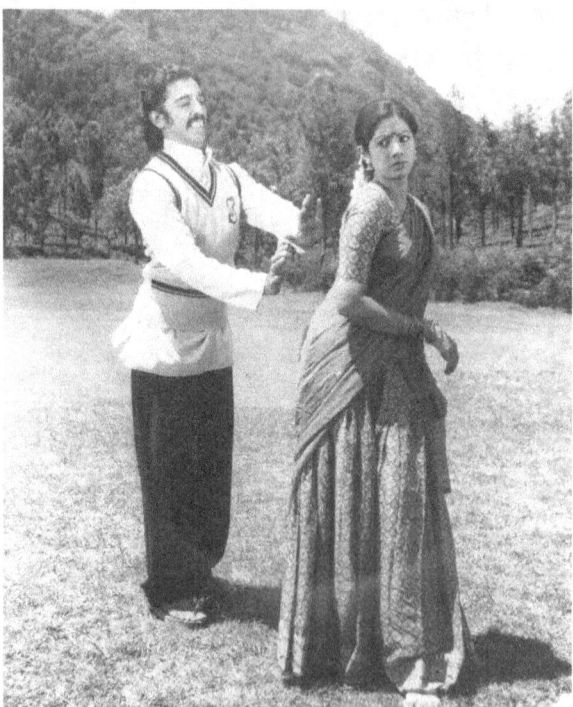

Top: A 14-year-old Sridevi with Rajinikanth in the dramatic and deeply disturbing Tamil film *Gayathri* (1977).

Bottom: Sridevi with Kamal Haasan in the 1979 Tamil comedy *Kalayanaraman.*

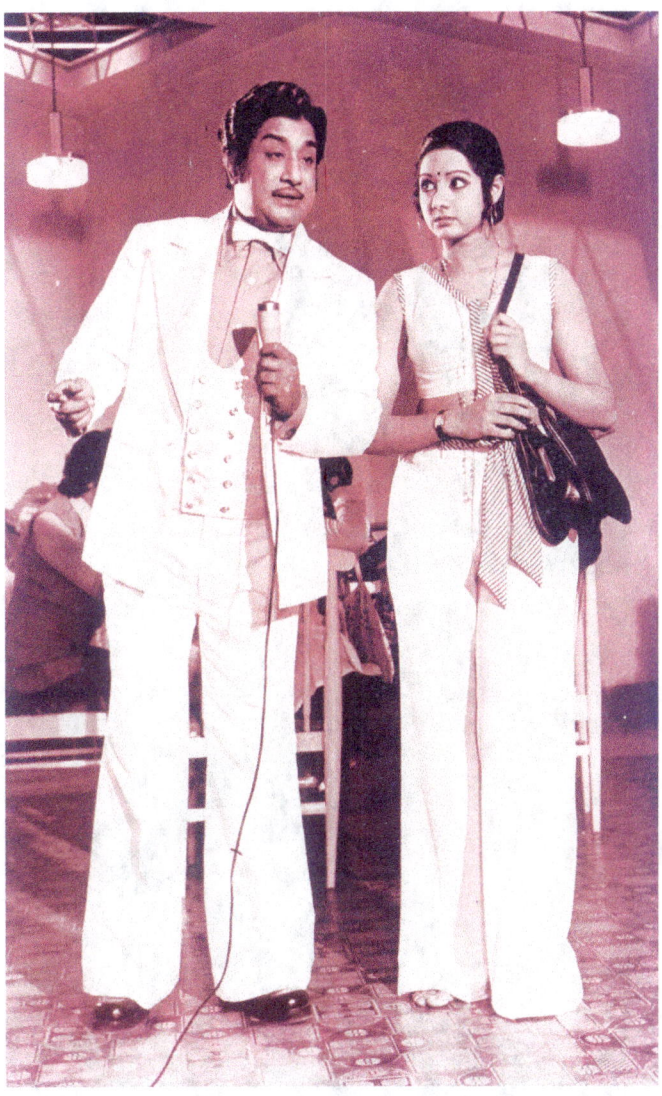

Sridevi with Sivaji Ganesan in 1979 Tamil drama *Kavari Maan*, where Ganesan essayed the role of Sridevi's father.

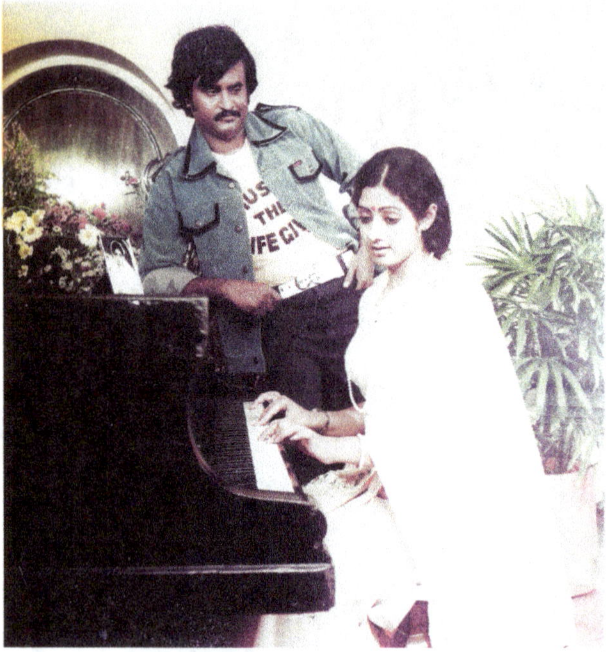

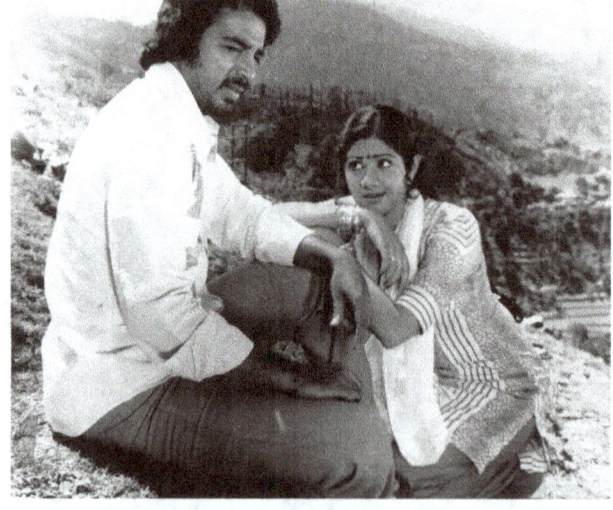

Top: Sridevi and Rajinikanth in the Tamil thriller *Johnny* (1980).

Bottom: Sridevi and Kamal Haasan in the Tamil drama *Varumayin Niram Sivappu* (1980), directed by K. Balachander.

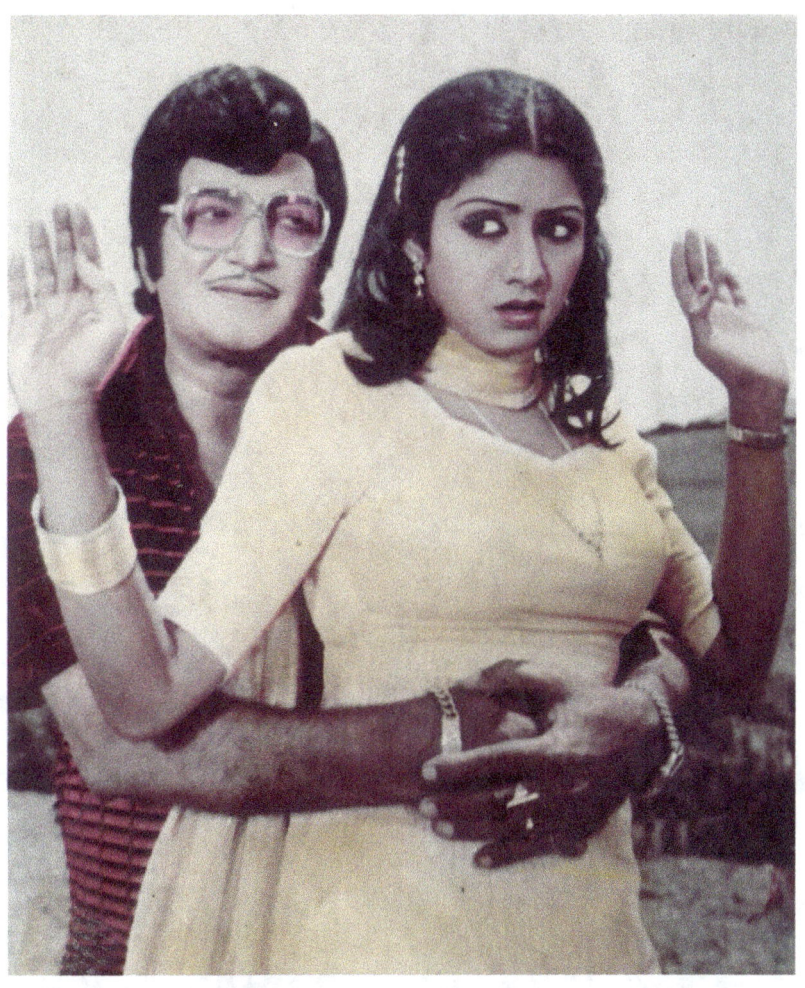

Sridevi being wooed by the peerless N.T. Rama Rao in the 1980 Telugu
action film *Aatagadu*.

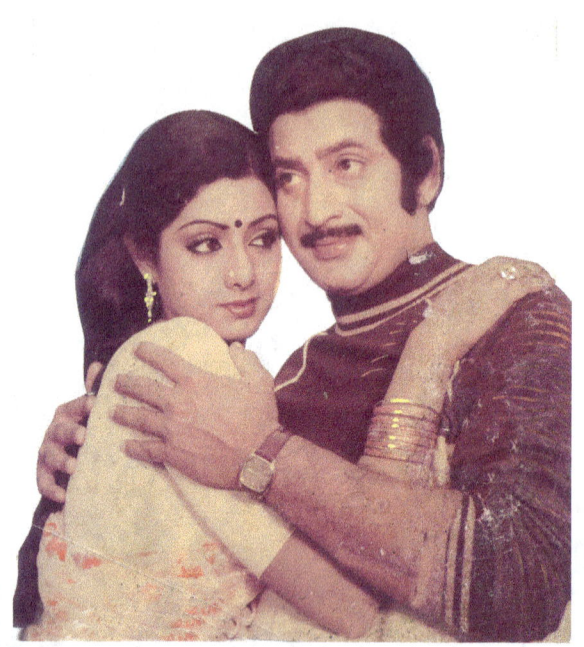

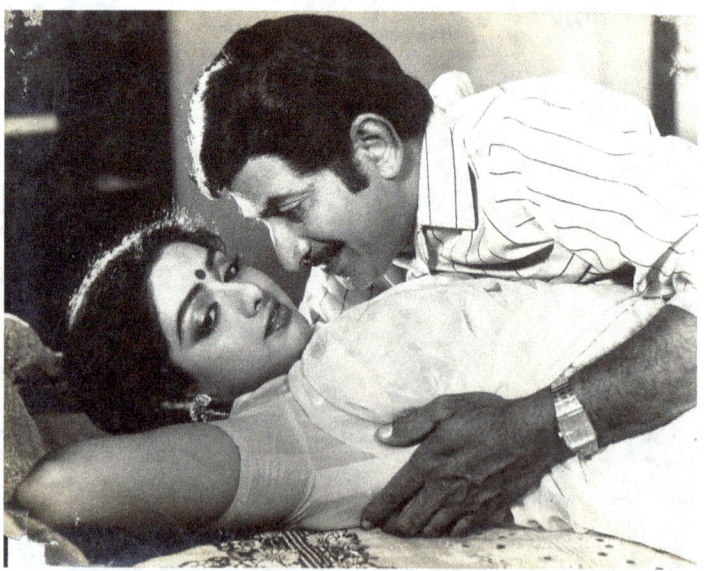

Top: Sridevi with Krishna in the 1982 Telugu drama *Kalavari Samasaram*. The two ended up working on 29 films as a romantic pairing.

Bottom: Krishna romancing Sridevi in the 1985 Telugu film *Pachani Kapuram*.

Eleven

The Years of Night and Lotus (I)

*R*ajini (Night) and *Kamal* (Lotus)...see what I did there?

I have mentioned earlier how Sridevi, Kamal Haasan and Rajinikanth were 'growing up' together. Kamal Haasan was already a superstar owing to his Malayalam (and later Tamil) films, but Rajinikanth hadn't become the 'Thalaivar' yet.

Sridevi did 18 films with Rajinikanth and 27 films with Kamal Haasan. With Kamal, she formed a popular on-screen romantic pair. They were a thing and people loved to see them together. But it all truly started with Malayalam movies. Between 1976 and 1977, they had featured in as many as five Malayalam films together: *Kuttavum Shikshayum* (1976), *Aadhya Paadam, Aasheervaadam, Sathyavan Savithri* and *Nirakudam* (all 1977). This kind of sudden spurt of prolificacy by this pair in Malayalam cinema is baffling. Many of these films, notably *Nirakudam*, were box-office hits. *Nirakudam* was remade from the Tamil classic *Bhaaga Pirivinai* (1959), which was also remade in Hindi as *Khandan* starring Sunil Dutt and Nutan. Sridevi reprised Nutan's role in the Malayalam film. Another piece that many talk about is a spectacular dance recital by Sridevi in *Sathyavan Savithri.* Even 'spectacular' as a word falls criminally short of describing what this 'untrained dancer' did there.

The first truly notable film of the Kamal–Sridevi pair was one in which they were not even romantically paired. *Manitharil Ithanai Nirangala* (1978) was one of those rare Indian films where a man and woman were principal characters in a movie but were not a romantic couple. The film opens with Shantha (Sridevi) trying to find a job in Madras. A man lures her into an 'interview' and forces himself on her. She is then at a police station, crying her heart out, but she's clubbed with a group of women arrested that day for sex work. They mistake her for a sex worker. One of the women takes a liking to her and gives her a place to stay. They become like sisters. But Shantha sees her benefactor being dragged out like a doormat by men. To help her and support her, Shantha tries to venture into sex work herself but a righteous old gentleman reprimands her. When the woman she lived with eventually dies, Shantha is on her own again. She returns to her village and starts living with her friend Devaki (Sathyapriya). Devaki's husband, Velu (Kamal Haasan), is a bit of an obnoxious prude but his heart is in the right place. Shantha's past returns to haunt her in the form of the cop who had arrested her before. The village station master (Murali Mohan) falls in love with Shantha. While she ponders whether to reciprocate, the station master's father turns out to be the same old man who once dissuaded her from sex work.

In Tamil cinema till then she wasn't quite the swinging star that she was in Telugu, but through this movie she was able to spread her wings. How much of these complex roles she could actually 'understand' at this stage is debatable but her performances were flawless. It is that indescribable superpower she had that books like this one and many others before this, have attempted to fathom.

The next Kamal–Sridevi outing was just as mainstream as *Manitharil Ithanai Nirangala*. Partly inspired from the 1945 Hollywood musical *Wonder Man, Kalyanaraman* (1979) is about a dead man returning from the grave to avenge his own death with the help of his identical twin. It was later remade in Bollywood as *Ghazab* (1982), with Dharmendra and Rekha playing the lead roles. Kamal Haasan got the author-backed role and Sridevi didn't have much to do, though by now she had acquired the art of making good use of her screen time even in unremarkable roles. This was something that held her in good stead throughout her Bollywood years. Having witnessed the murder of Kamal Haasan's character, her character loses her mental balance. There are scenes that bring to mind her histrionics in *Sadma/Moondram Pirai*, which was still three years away then.

Neela Malargal (1979) was the second remake of *Anuraag* that Sridevi starred in, after her adult debut *Anuragalu*, only this time it was in Tamil instead of Telugu. There were many embellishments in the story which made it different from the original film. Additionally, *Thayillamal Nannilai* has gone down in history as the only film that had a peacock uniting the hero and heroine (Kamal and Sridevi). The film also brought the trio (of Kamal, Sridevi and Rajinikanth) together again, if only for a few minutes since Rajinikanth was playing a cameo. Sridevi and Kamal were on a roll, as they became a bankable romantic pair on-screen. Many of these films were successful, with films like *Guru* (1980) which were major blockbusters. And it was not just any two actors. Both of these people were powerful performers, and they were in their prime. When they shared a frame, it was like talent and charisma oozing out of the screen. I.V. Sasi, who had done as many as nine Malayalam films with Sridevi, directed her in *Guru*. The film was almost a frame-to-frame remake of Pramod Chakraborty's 1973 Hindi superhit *Jugnu*, with Kamal and Sridevi reprising Dharmendra and Hema Malini's roles respectively. The films were so similar that even the dialogues and the shots were near-identical. Except Dharmendra's hat was replaced by Kamal's terrible toupee. It was one of Sridevi and Kamal Haasan's biggest hits.

K. Balachander, Kamal's revered KB Sir, was Sridevi and Rajinikanth's mentor too. When he asked Kamal to mentor the young girl, there was no question of him not doing it. Kamal was almost like an elder sibling, teaching her things since the parent had instructed him to do so. The two struck a chord, and the chemistry was evident on-screen. They later come back together for their mentor in *Varumayin Niram Sivappu* (1980), which loosely translates to 'the colour of poverty is red'.

As the title would imply, the film has somewhat leftist leanings. A band of unemployed Tamil boys, led by Rangan (Kamal Haasan) live in a cheap tenement in Delhi and try to navigate the time between unemployment and life beginning. He meets Devi (Sridevi), another youngster just like them who is trying to eke out a living by acting in theatre. The heart of the film lies in the cynicism of the unemployed youth of the 1970s, but is dealt with caustic humour. Much like an adolescent sitting in the toilet with forbidden magazines, one of the boys sits around in the pot with a newspaper open on his lap—dreaming of himself sitting in an office doing mundane office work. When Devi insists that they finish their lunch, the perpetually hungry boys put up a show with empty pans to make her believe they are having the meal of their lives. Kamal as the disillusioned youth spouts lines written by the legendary Tamil poet Subramania Bharathi. Sridevi plays a simple middle-class woman, a far cry from the glamour queens she was destined to play out repeatedly in the Hindi film industry. She has hopes and dreams like all girls her age, but her parasite of a father who lives on her money proves to be the bane of her existence. There's a Hindi song in the movie 'Tu Hai Raja', which was probably Sridevi's first full-length Hindi song in a movie featuring her as the heroine. It was also most likely the first Hindi song to be featured in a mainstream Tamil movie. The lyrics were written by the doyen of Tamil playback singing, P.B. Sreenivas. Sridevi and Kamal's characters have some priceless moments in the film, including one where he is 'looking for socialism' in a garbage dump as she looks on in amusement. *Varumayin Niram Sivappu* was shot simultaneously in Telugu as *Aakali Rajyam* and released a year later. In 1983, Balachander directed a Hindi version called *Zara Si Zindagi* with Kamal reprising his role but Sridevi was replaced with Anita Raj. That film stood on its own, with lines written by Gulzar and Balachander adding some exclusive bits which were not in the original. For instance, the postbox (one of those red-box ones where you dropped 'letters' to be posted back in the day) started laughing every time one of the boys (played by Arjun Chakraborty) tried to post a job application. While the Tamil film became a landmark, it's a pity that the Hindi version didn't work.

Meendum Kokila (1981) is another prime example of how far Sridevi had come as a performer. She plays a Brahmin housewife named Kokila. Kamal plays the husband, Mani, a

motormouth of a lawyer with a roving eye and a tendency
to get touchy-feely at the slightest pretext. Mani strikes a
friendship with an actress called Kamini (Deepa) and lies
through his teeth to find an opportunity to spend time with
her. The two develop an intimacy. Kokila comes to know of
this and resolves to win her man back at any cost.

Sridevi nails the role of the quintessential middle-class
Brahmin housewife, including wearing the *madisar* (a
particular style in which Tamil Brahmin women drape their
saris) throughout. In fact, there's a scene in which she is
asked to teach Kamini how to wear a madisar sari for a role
the latter has to play. Mani (Kamal) can't resist the sight of
Kamini's midriff and proceeds to touch it inappropriately.
Understandably, Kokila throws a fit. Mani explains it away,
saying he had thought it was Kokila instead. Sridevi handles
this role with aplomb, playing a small-town girl who can
transform from a naive housewife to a badass woman at a
moment's notice.

Rekha was supposed to play the role of Kamini and
the film was supposed to be directed by J. Mahendran, a
revered filmmaker in the Tamil pantheon. Rekha even shot
a few reels and was part of some promotional photoshoots,
all of which can be found online. It would have been her
only film in Tamil. But for some reason, she walked out
of the project and was replaced by Deepa (also known as
Unni Mary). Mahendran also quit the project. There were
many apocryphal stories surrounding the exit, but nothing
was ever substantiated.

Meendum Kokila is filled with moments where Sridevi
sparkles in her ability to not just gesticulate at high points,
but also use the nuances and gestures that embellish good
performances. Regardless of the serious subject of marital
infidelity, the film is presented as a comedy. It starts with

the marriage of the lead pair and is filled with tongue-in-cheek moments between Sridevi, Kamal and their little daughter. And in terms of performance, Sridevi dances toe-to-toe with Kamal Haasan. The film was a humongous success and Sridevi was heaped with praise. She also won her first Filmfare Award for best actress (Tamil) for the film. The lilting music was by the maestro Ilaiyaraaja. The song 'Chinna Chiru Vayathil' is one of the highlights of the film. When Sridevi (voiced by P. Sushila) forgets her lines, Kamal (voiced by K.J. Yesudas) picks up and an old lady grinds nuts in the background. That pounding noise slowly weaves into the beats of the song.

If *Meendum Kokila* was about Kamal duping Sridevi's character to flirt with another woman, *Vazhve Mayam* (1982) shows him obsessed with winning her attention. It is a remake of her earlier Telugu film *Premabhishekam*, where it's ANR who is pining for her. *Vazhve Mayam* was part of Sridevi's initial foray into playing the glamorous object of desire. It was the kind of film where she just had to flutter about, looking pretty. But she did the pretty-young-thing act as effortlessly as the naive housewife. Raja (Kamal) is a compulsive flirt but when he sees Devi (Sridevi), his heart skips a beat or two. Devi is in no mood to reciprocate and his constant efforts to win her over only make her angrier with each passing day. Eventually when she does give in to his charms, he finds out that he has cancer. Now his struggle is to keep away the woman that he moved heaven and earth to be close to. From there, it's all downhill.

Vazhve Mayam had Sridevi and Kamal do the dance-and-song routines they were hitherto not seen doing. The film was a quintessential 1980s love story and ended up being one of the biggest blockbusters of the Kamal–Sridevi pair. And here too Sridevi danced toe-to-toe with Kamal Haasan, quite literally this time. 'Mazhai Kaala Megam Oondru' was the dance-with-abandon-and-the-world-be-damned kind of a song, and Kamal–Sridevi were a sight for sore eyes.

Kamal Haasan later wrote in his weekly series of writings in the Tamil magazine *Ananda Vikatan*: 'Those days, couples (at weddings) were compared to us, saying they looked like Kamal and Sridevi. They must have seen us singing duets and hugging. We hid the truth (about the nature of the relationship) so as to not shatter that dream.'[26] Kamal and Sridevi were really like brother and sister. As mentioned earlier, their mentor Balachander once tasked him to groom her. They were doing so many films together that Kamal said he used to wonder 'her again?' when he heard about the casting. Kamal also said in the India Today Conclave in 2018:

> I don't know when Sridevi grew up. I knew her as a child. And I almost was dismissive. I was given the task of being with Sridevi, to break her in into acting. I was myself a novice, but I was a few classes (in acting school) ahead of her. But she caught up with double promotion and we were paired. She had a bag of tricks. She knew how to make a permutation-combination of it. Even those who taught her that, wouldn't know that it came from there. That's the beauty of that girl. It is so strange... She always, always addressed me as Sir. That's the relationship we had. I was her class pupil leader. That's all![27]

---

[26]'When Sridevi, Kamal Hid Truth about Their Relationship for Couples Compared to Them', *Deccan Chronicle*, 2 March 2018, https://tinyurl. com/44zu9nwm. Accessed on 29 May 2023.

[27]'Kamal Haasan Remembers Sridevi On The India Today Conclave Stage', YouTube, https://tinyurl.com/4h3442wx. Accessed on 8 June 2023.

It was this relationship that came to the fore in their most abiding work together—the Tamil film *Moondram Pirai* (1982). Balu Mahendra, as a young cinematographer, had witnessed the adolescent Sridevi try to pull off the role of a grown-up in *Anuragalu* (1975). He was married to a young actress called Shobha at the time. In 1980, Shobha died by suicide. And like it always happens when a young person dies, the media went into a tizzy. Though Mahendra was not really blamed for it, he had his own mechanism to cope. Shobha's acting career began much like Sridevi, as a toddling little three-year-old. Then there were 70-odd films in four languages, a National Award and two Filmfare awards for acting—all within a rather short span of 17 years. Balu Mahendra poured his memories of a life spent with his wife into the heart-wrenching story of *Moondram Pirai*, literally meaning 'the third crescent'. This was Mahendra's fourth directorial venture and his first without his muse, Shobha, featuring in it.

In the movie, Srinivas or 'Cheenu' (Kamal Haasan) comes across Vijaya or Viji (Sridevi) in a brothel and is consumed with affection for her when he realizes that she is like an overgrown child, kidnapped and entrapped against her will. He flees with her to the quaint little hill station he calls home. They build their own little cocoon, sheltered from the outside world. Viji learns to completely rely on Cheenu and he does the same. He attends to her and cares for her, and soon they both take over each other's lives. However, it comes to light that she is not Vijaya but Bhagyalakshmi, who got involved in a freak accident that wiped out her memory and turned her mental age to that of a child.

The music of the film, done by Ilaiyaraaja, was particularly evocative. This one was for the ages. Especially the number called 'Poongatru Puthiraanathu', an exquisite track which was later modified and included in *Sadma* as the ever-so-evocative 'Ae Zindagi Gale Lagaa Le'. The tunes are similar yet noticeably different. If the Hindi lyrics by Gulzar were like a ray of sunshine on a winter afternoon, the original lyrics by Kannadasan were like a river which went looking for the sea. The tune of the Hindi version was later used in the Rajinikanth–Madhavi starrer *Thambikku Entha Ooru* in the song 'En Vazhvile Varum Anbe Vaa'. *Moondram Pirai* was Kannadasan's last work as a lyricist, because he passed away soon after. It is ironic that the Kaviarasu who was responsible for starting Sridevi's movie career, delivered his swansong for a film that featured her as a heroine.

It wasn't probably as difficult for Sridevi to tap into the child in her. She was 19 at that time, technically still a teenager. There were certain childish affectations in her performances. She used to flutter her eyelids a certain way, puff up her cheeks and speak in a cutesy manner that could turn mountains into marshmallows. In *Moondram Pirai*, she went back to this particular affectation which she had employed just a decade ago as a child artist. And it worked spectacularly. The sibling equation that she shared with Kamal must have come in handy here. If the stunning climax belonged to Kamal Haasan, the rest of the film was about Sridevi churning out the performance of her lifetime and making Kamal's last act all the more heartbreaking.

At the behest of their mentor, K. Balachander, Kamal had earlier taken this little girl under his—rather formidable—wing. That girl now had wings of her own.

Moondram Pirai was remade in Hindi the following year by Balu Mahendra himself. Other than altering a few songs and some cast members, *Sadma* (1983) was practically the same film. It had a similar impact on Bollywood audiences as their Tamil counterparts. It is part of movie folklore now.

The last film that Sridevi and Kamal Haasan worked in together was a Telugu film called *Oka Radha Iddaru Krishnulu* (1986), which was dubbed in Tamil as *Hare Radha Hare Krishna.*

Kamal Haasan, while reminiscing about Sridevi at the MAMI (Mumbai Academy of Moving Images) Film Festival 2018, said: 'We liked each other. Her mother liked me a lot. She used to tell me, "Why don't you marry her?" And I'd say, "Oh no! It'd be like marrying within the family."'[28]

Unlike Kamal Haasan and Sridevi, Rajinikanth's relationship with her wasn't that of a senior or a sibling. She was a peer. When he was struggling to gain a foothold through roles in films like *Apoorva Raagangal, Moondru Mudichu* and *Pathinaru Vayathinile,* Sridevi was already something of a star.

Much like Shatrughan Sinha in Hindi films, Rajinikanth was playing negative roles and still getting applause from the audiences. When he beat the hero, the crowd cheered for him. This was still during the phase when both Kamal and Rajinikanth, untarnished by superstardom, were experimenting with different kind of roles. While Bollywood stars like Aamir Khan and Akshay Kumar started pushing the envelope once they attained a certain level of stardom, with Kamal and Rajinikanth it was the exact opposite. They started off with the unconventional films. When *Gayathri* (1977) released, the producer Panchu Arunachalam dragged writer Sujatha to the theatre to show her the movie. When they noticed Rajinikanth—the villain of the piece—was getting so much attention, they realized that he was made to be the hero.

---

[28]'Kamal Haasan Reflects on Sridevi's Career, Marriage Proposal and Legacy', *The Biggest Sridevi Fan Page*, 20 February 2020, https://tinyurl.com/4p9pcetf. Accessed on 8 June 2023.

The very next year, Rajinikanth was roped in to play the hero in another story written by Sujatha. He was hired for the same role that the hero in *Gayathri*, Jaishankar, was playing.

Twelve

The Years of Night and Lotus (II)

Writer Sujatha Rangarajan was an incredibly prolific author of Tamil short stories and novels. One of the more popular franchises he created was of a team of two do-gooder lawyers by the name of Ganesh and Vasanth. In the book, Ganesh is an advocate and Vasanth is his junior. Across 15 novels and a bunch of short stories, Sujatha depicted the two of them solving crimes in various situations. *Gayathri* (1977) was the first film where this duo was shown. The role of Ganesh was played by Jaishankar, while Rajinikanth played the villain. One year later, there was another adaptation of a Ganesh–Vasanth novel. The producer of *Gayathri*, Panchu Arunachalam, was once again collaborating with the author Sujatha. And this time, Rajinikanth got to play the role of Ganesh. The film was *Priya* (1978), based on the novel of the same name. Sridevi played the female lead.

Priya was made in both Tamil and Kannada, so it also became Sridevi's second Kannada film as a heroine. The first was *Hennu Samsarada Kannu* (1975). In this maudlin family drama, a perfect daughter-in-law and wife (Manjula) becomes the target of her husband's (Srinath) ire because of how popular she is becoming with his parents and sister (Sridevi). *Hennu Samsarada Kannu* was Sridevi's second film as a 'grown-up' actress. She was 13 at that time. And even here, like most of the projects that she was a part of, Sridevi was exposed to some of the luminaries of Kannada cinema. Take K.S. Ashwath, for instance. Ashwath was an incredibly talented actor who aced key character roles in over 300 films in a span of a little more than half a century (from 1955 to 2007). There was also T.N. Balakrishna, who had a hearing impairment and worked by lip-reading his colleagues' dialogues. Even then his acting skills were of the highest order. In the same film Sridevi also shared screen space with Manorama, a Tamilian who worked in almost all the major film industries including Hindi. She was a staggeringly prolific actress who worked in more than 1,500 movies.

Priya is about a young actress—much like Sridevi herself—who is pushed around by a producer, her 'godfather'. This man wants nothing less than to have control over her career. She is in love with Bharath (Ambareesh) but the producer, Janardhan, does not approve. So, she hires the services of Ganesh to release her from the producer's clutches. Rajinikanth gets to play Julius Caesar briefly and Sridevi wears a swimsuit for the first time. No harm done. There was much hoopla over the fact that *Priya* was shot in Singapore, one of the earliest Kannada films to do so. But just like all their films till this point, Sridevi and Rajinikanth were not a romantic pair in the film. Sridevi was paired opposite Ambareesh—one of Kannada cinema's most promising stars who was then two years away from his breakout role as an undercover cop in *Antha*. All three lead actors involved in *Priya* were at the cusp of greatness. But if acting calibre were the sole parameter, Sridevi had already touched greatness.

As I have tried to demonstrate through this book, much before she became *the* Sridevi—years before she sat pretty on the throne of Bollywood—she had already done some of the best work of her life.

But Kannada was probably the only South Indian language Sridevi wasn't comfortable speaking on-screen—or at least it would appear so. Her voice in *Hennu Samsarada Kannu* was dubbed over by another actress, although just a year before she had spoken her own dialogues in *Bhakta Kumbara* (where she was cast with Kannada superstar Dr Rajkumar). It can be assumed that all she was doing was mugging up her lines, but in *Hennu Samsarada Kannu* she was playing the hero Srinath's sister which required some complex dialogue delivery. This may have caused her to dub with a different voice. And the same is true for *Priya*, where although she dubbed for herself in the Tamil version, someone else dubbed for her in Kannada. There is a scene where she has to hum a line to impress a film producer (Major Sundarrajan in the Tamil version/K. Ashwath in Kannada). In the Tamil version, Sridevi breaks into a jig and sings in her own voice.

S.P. Muthuraman, the director of *Priya*, had debuted with *Kanimuthu Paappa* which featured Sridevi as a child actor. They were reuniting as a director and heroine after a gap of just six years. Muthuraman had become a force to reckon with by then. He was the first to cast Rajinikanth in a positive role in *Bhuvana Oru Kelvikkuri* (1977), which was the beginning of an association spanning 25-odd films.

So far, Rajinikanth had played Sridevi's tormentor (*Pathinaru Vayathinile*), stepson (*Moondru Mudichu*), evil husband (*Gayathri*), brother (*Kavikkuyil*) and lawyer (*Priya*). But it was in *Vanakkatukuriya Kathaliye* (1978) that they first played lovers and how!

In the movie, there's a miniature sphinx just a little taller than her in front of which she shimmies and sings: 'I am queen of queens!'. The sphinx parts and he steps out, announcing, 'Hey, you know me. I am king of kings!' That's how Sridevi and Rajinikanth's entry song, 'Kottu Kottu Melam, Thattu Thattu Thaalam' begins. Sridevi dances with wild abandon, and Rajinikanth plays along. They are Jenny and Joe, and they are very much in love. But unbeknownst to Jenny, she has an identical twin called Shanthi who has extrasensory powers due to an accident. When Shanthi makes some predictions that come true, the simple folk of her town immediately perceive her as a goddess and worship her with deep devotion. Shanthi, an ardently religious person, finds this blasphemy unbearable. Jenny fights battles of her own when she finds out that she has cancer.

Almost every other Tamil film in this period seemed to be giving Sridevi an opportunity to showcase her histrionics. Unlike her early stints in Bollywood, here she was being given author-backed roles. In *Vanakkatukuriya Kathaliye* too, she gets ample opportunities to do what she does best. Shanthi's frustration, Jenny's illness...Sridevi depicts them with the artfulness of a seasoned actor. There are scenes with Jenny writhing in agony where you want to reach out and comfort her. Rajinikanth as Joe plays the helpless lover who has to see his sweetheart suffer. The chemistry between the two of them here is good, but they were still a couple of years away from their best work together.

Director J. Mahendran was widely known for redefining Tamil cinema through his oeuvre. He achieved this with just 12 films in a career spanning 28 years. He had a distinctive style that set him apart from his peers. His approach was characterized by a tenderness for storytelling and for his characters, but it rarely became maudlin. The camera seemed to be caressing the subjects. In this, Mahendran was ably supported by his cinematographer Ashok Kumar Aggarwal[29]. Mahendran and Ashok Kumar made some gorgeous-looking films, including *Nenjathai Killathe, Nandu, Metti, Kai Kodukkam Kai,* etc. But their crowning glory as a team was *Johnny* (1980), an exquisitely beautiful film filled with priceless moments one would like to frame and store for eternity. It is also Rajinikanth and Sridevi's best film together.

Johnny (Rajinikanth) is a suave conman with a silver tongue, who makes a living by hoodwinking people. His goal though is to pay off his father's debts—a father who barely acknowledged his mother and him as family, until he fell on hard times. Johnny also has a penchant for music and he is especially enamoured by a popular singer called Archana (Sridevi). There's a song called 'Oru Iniya Manathu Isaiya Anaithu Sellam', which can be loosely translated as 'a sweet mind will carry the music into a flood of pleasure'. Sridevi sings on the stage as Rajinikanth watches from the audience. You know it's Sujatha's voice, but Sridevi fools you into believing it's really her who's doing the singing. She cranes her neck and breaks into a smile. Then she looks away and hums. When the song is over, like Johnny in the audience, the viewer is busy collecting their heart from the floor. The Sridevi of *Chandni,* of *Lamhe,* was up there on the stage. But in those films, her charm was enveloped by the need to be animated. Here, the stillness she achieves in her performance is breathtaking.

As Archana and Johnny get to know each other better, they reach a point where both feel the need to take their relationship to the next level. But unlike most other films

---

[29]Aggarwal was the son of a Hindi poet from Allahabad who came to Madras to learn filmmaking at the Institute of Film Technology, and then stayed back for life.

of the time, Archana makes the first move. For a 1980s mainstream film this was quite remarkable, even shocking. Most Indian films of the era carefully toed the line when it came to gender stereotypes. The only exceptions were the envelope-pushing 'art films', a domain that didn't exist in Tamil cinema. While staying within the framework of mainstream entertainers, skilled filmmakers like Mahendran were breaking stereotypes. Archana clearly asks Johnny if he'd like to marry her. When Johnny hesitates, she thinks he is turning her down because she is a stage performer. He hasn't yet told her that he is a conman and this bugs him. Although he had not accounted for love, it is impossible for him to not surrender to her.

Johnny has a doppelgänger by the name of Vidyasagar, a quirky barber who lives among his poultry and his flower plants. In a fit of rage, he guns down his unfaithful lover and the man she is involved with. He is all over the news and people start mistaking Johnny for him. Vidyasagar, who is on the run from the cops, lands up at Archana's door. Archana from *Johnny* is one of Sridevi's most fascinating roles. Her restrained, measured performance was a far cry from her Hindi and Telugu films. This makes one wonder why she wasn't employed by 'serious' Bollywood filmmakers, like Hrishikesh Mukherjee, Basu Chatterjee and Shyam Benegal.

Dharma Yuddham—an action film directed by R.C. Sakthi that established Rajinikanth as a superstar—was another major commercial blockbuster of this phase, and a significant success for both Sridevi and Rajinikanth. Vijay's (Rajinikanth) parents are killed by the maniacal Robert (Thengai Srinivasan) on a full-moon night. Since then, on every full-moon night Vijay goes stark raving mad. During this sudden bout, he has to be chained to a bed to keep him from hurting others. It's often called a 'medical thriller' but the premise is an entirely superstitious concept. The supposed impact of the moon on human sanity is an age-old grandma's tale—hence the word lunatic, which connects back to lunar cycles. The fact that it has zero basis in science is obvious. But the film takes it seriously. In the climax—obviously, on a full-moon night—Vijay acquires superhuman strength and tears the bad guys to shreds. Sridevi plays Chitra, an enterprising newspaper reporter who hounds Vijay (a very busy business magnate, apparently) for an interview. He keeps rebuffing her. She even scales the wall of his bungalow and lands on his garden (foreshadowing the real-life paparazzi who would chase her in the years to come). Sridevi, with the sari draped around her, throws her chappals to the other side and climbs the wall like it is an everyday thing. When Rajinikanth shoos her away yet again, she begrudgingly leaves the same way she came. They play a bittersweet game of one-upmanship. He tries to put her out, but she bounces back each time finding a way to make her presence felt. Finally, when they fall for each other it seems organic. Though a far cry from *Johnny*, Sridevi's role in *Dharma Yuddham* was not of the standard arm-candy heroine role seen in most action films. There was grit, determination and a lot of fire. Director R.C. Sakthi had also given her a meaty role in *Manidharil Ithanai Nirangala* just a year earlier.

If the films with Rajinikanth and Kamal were raking in the moolah, her films with other Tamil stars were also gaining box-office favour. After having worked with Sivaji Ganesan (on *Babu*, *Vasantha Maligai* and *Bharatha Vilas*) as a child star, Sridevi continued to play his daughter in *Pilot Premnath* (1978) and *Kavari Maan* (1979). In *Pilot Premnath*— a maudlin family drama that remains a popular classic— Sridevi plays Sivaji's visually challenged daughter. Premnath loses his wife in a domestic accident and raises his three children single-handedly. An old letter written by his late wife surfaces, which reveals that one of his three children is not theirs. This fills Premnath with rage. He assembles his children and breaks into a song, 'Who is the Black Sheep?' The director for this was A.C. Tirulokchandar, who had earlier directed Sivaji and Sridevi in *Babu*. This was during the intervening years before she successfully graduated to adult roles. Sridevi recycles the cute, innocent daughter act that she had mastered by then. She had earlier played a blind girl in the Malayalam film *Swapnangal* (1970) and in the Telugu film *Anuragalu* (1975). As the pilot's favourite child, Kanchan, she gets a more significant role—more so because she is revealed to be the 'Black Sheep'.

The very next year Sridevi played Sivaji Ganesan's daughter again in *Kavari Maan*, while in *Pattakathi Bhairavan* she played his stepsister. Little Uma of *Kavari Maan* witnesses her father bludgeon her mother to death before her very eyes. The father (Sivaji) ends up in jail and she grows up associating the word 'father' with this violent act. His brother, Rangarajan (Major Sundarrajan), raises her and Uma believes her uncle to be her father. When her father is released from jail and faces the grown-up Uma, the trauma resurfaces. The rest of the film concerns itself with how he wins her back. In these early films with Sivaji, Sridevi managed to bag some meaty roles even as his sister or daughter. But by 1980, just a year after *Kavari Maan*, she started playing Sivaji Ganesan's heroine.

In 1976, the reigning superstar of Hindi cinema, Amitabh Bachchan played the dual role of an ageing gangster and his wayward son in the film *Adalat*. Like most of his films in the 1970s, this one hit the jackpot. Throughout that decade and the one following it, a curious phenomenon emerged in Tamil cinema. Tamil superstars like MGR, Sivaji

Ganesan and Rajinikanth (the latter more than the formers) were remaking Amitabh Bachchan films by the dozen. The popularity of these films and the power of the Salim–Javed brand of storytelling, had travelled to the South. Since Hindi films were not seen there in large numbers, the opportunity to remake these films into Tamil seemed too good to pass up. In the remake of *Zanjeer*, MGR played both Bachchan's as well as Pran's character in a bizarre double role. Throughout the 1980s, Rajinikanth reprised Bachchan roles in film after film: *Deewar* as *Thee*, *Trishul* as *Mr Bharath* and the most successful franchise of them all, *Don* as *Billa*. Sivaji Ganesan starred in relatively fewer remakes, like that of *Majboor* (*Naan Vazhavaippen*) and *Muqaddar ka Sikandar* (*Amara Kaaviyam*). Sridevi was Sivaji's lead heroine in two such films: *Vishwaroopam* (a remake of *Adalat*) and *Sandhippu* (inspired from *Naseeb*).

In *Vishwaroopam*, Sridevi played the 'younger' Sivaji's girlfriend. The casting probably was meant to reinforce the 'youth' of his character. Curiously, there is a whole conversation between the two conducted entirely in English. She appears when 70 per cent of the movie is done, foreshadowing the kind of roles she would be known for in her Telugu film oeuvre. In *Sandhippu*, she definitely had more screen time and was reinterpreting the part portrayed by Hema Malini in *Naseeb*. The film literally starts (after an extended pre-credits sequence) with Sridevi going the whole hog with a glittering outfit, sashaying to 'Raathiri Nilaavil Ragasiya Kanaavil'. This was 1983 and she was still a good four years away from 'Hawa Hawai' but that's the kind of imagery this song conjures up. Sivaji, again portraying a father–son duo, plays Pran's as well as Amitabh Bachchan's role from *Naseeb*. His son Prabhu played Rishi Kapoor's role. The real-life father and son were effectively playing brothers.

Sivaji Ganesan was already a senior actor when Sridevi worked as a child actress with him in *Babu*. In *Sandhippu*, he's pushing 55 and she's in her prime. But these things never bothered her. If you look at her eyes in *Sandhippu*, you want to believe that she was madly in love with Raja.

Sridevi was now closer to the persona that eventually became her calling card in Hindi cinema. All these years, she had been learning from her seniors. But now, she had learned the art of stealing the show—pulling the rug right from beneath the feet of those very legends.

Thirteen

The Malayalam Sophomore

Most of the Malayali film buffs and critics I tried to reach out to seemed to be of the opinion that Sridevi didn't have many Malayalam films worth talking about. They were hard-pressed to recall any of her films made in the language. But consider this. Sridevi won her first ever award for a Malayalam film. *Poompatta*, which we have discussed at length in a previous chapter, won her the Kerala Film Award for best child artist. Before breaking out as a superhit on-screen couple in Tamil cinema with *Sigappu Rojakkal*, Kamal Haasan and Sridevi had also worked in at least five Malayalam films together.

In Tamil filmdom, directors like K. Balachander, S.P. Muthuraman and A.C. Tirulokchandar helped in shaping her world and taught her many a thing. In Telugu, K. Raghavendra Rao not only mentored her but put her on the path to national recognition and stardom. Likewise in Malayalam cinema, illustrious filmmaker Irruppam Veedu Sasidaran or I.V. Sasi was her mentor. Among the four states that comprise the South Indian film industries, Kerala is known for its affinity to serious cinema. While filmmakers like Adoor Gopalakrishnan and G. Aravindan were breaking new

ground in art-house cinema, I.V. Sasi and his ilk were pushing
the boundaries of narrative storytelling while staying within
the confines of 'commercial' cinema. One of the subjects
I.V. Sasi is known to have dealt with is sexuality, which has
been a taboo in Indian cinema since the very beginning.

When Sridevi and Sasi collaborated for the first time,
he had directed just two films. *Aalinganam* (1976) was when
they worked together for the first time. They then continued
to collaborate in nine more films in the next four years.
Raghavan, who starred opposite Sridevi in the film, later
said: 'Sasi had already told me that the little girl would be
my heroine. We were all curious to see her. I already knew
her as Murugan in *Kumara Sambhavam*, and had watched
in disbelief her performance alongside stalwarts like Sivaji
Ganesan and Gemini Ganesan.'[30]

By the mid-1970s, just about the time she was transitioning
into adult roles, Sridevi had become quite the cult figure
in the South Indian film fraternity. Everybody knew about
this girl who was maddeningly prolific in all four industries,
working alongside legends, and who had now successfully
become a heroine. Even the great Kamal Haasan, who had
a similar transition from child actor to adult star, hadn't
appeared in as many films (across so many languages) as
Sridevi. Another thing that enhanced the aura around her
was her facility for languages, even as an adolescent. She
was fluent in Telugu because of her family and in Tamil
because she grew up in Chennai. But Malayalam and Kannada
were alien to her. While her lines in Kannada were dubbed
over, her Malayalam dialogues were all delivered by her
as a child artist. As a heroine though, her voice in all her

---

[30]Ayyapan, R., '"Little Girl Sridevi Charmed All of Us", Says Her First Malayalam
Co-star', *Deccan Chronicle*, 26 February 2018, https://tinyurl.com/2srjes4u.
Accessed on 19 May 2023.

early Malayalam films was dubbed over. But that doesn't take away from the fact that she was barely a teenager and already playing complex characters.

Like Sivaji Ganesan, MGR and Gemini Ganesan in Tamil cinema; ANR, NTR and Krishna in Telugu cinema; and Dr Rajkumar in Kannada, the first superstar in Malayalam cinema was Prem Nazir. In *Thulavarsham* (1976), Sridevi was granted the opportunity to work with Nazir. Raghavan was her first romantic lead in Malayalam. On the sets of I.V. Sasi's *Aalinganam*, as Raghavan described later, everyone was waiting to meet this little 'star' heroine. Sridevi, just 13 years old, had a childlike aura and won over everybody on the set. 'She charmed all of us. She was very sweet, ever smiling, like any innocent little girl,' Raghavan explained.[31] But she had already tasted stardom as a heroine with *Pathinaru Vayathinile,* and the small insecurities that plague every new starlet had started showing. Raghavan said, 'The only sign that indicated that ambition was stirring inside was her constant complaint about her nose. [...] She thought it was not good. We, especially Sasi, kept assuring her that her nose was beautiful. But she never seemed convinced.'[32]

Aalinganam released in 1976 and was a roaring success. All of a sudden, Sridevi had Malayalam producers eating out of her hands. In 1977, she had as many as 11 releases in Malayalam. I.V. Sasi directed six of these. The rest were helmed by illustrious filmmakers like Adoor Bhasi (a much-celebrated supporting actor, also known for his directorial work) and A. Bhimsingh (known mostly for his Tamil and Hindi films. He directed iconic Hindi films like Dilip Kumar's *Aadmi* and *Gopi*). In *Amme Anupame* she teamed up with K.S.

---

[31]Ibid.
[32]Ibid.

Sethumadhavan who had directed her, just two years before this, in her second Hindi film *Julie*. 1977 was also the year in which Sridevi collaborated with another upcoming star of Malayalam cinema—Kamal Haasan. Kamal has mentioned in multiple interviews that he experienced stardom first in Malayalam, and then in his home state of Tamil Nadu. *Kanyakumari* (1974) was his breakout role in Malayalam, opposite Rita Bhaduri (who later made a name for herself playing supporting roles in Bollywood films of the 1980s and '90s). Throughout the 1970s, Kamal did a number of Malayalam films that consolidated his stardom. In 1977, he and Sridevi appeared in as many as four Malayalam films: *Aadhya Paadam*, *Aasheervaadam*, *Sathyavan Savithri* and *Nirakudam*.

Nirakudam had Sridevi and Kamal play an earthy romantic pair—a precursor to what they were going to portray more successfully later that year in *Pathinaru Vayathinile*. Much like in the Tamil film, Kamal played a man with a disability in *Nirakudam* and Sridevi played the woman who loves and protects him. But that's where the similarities with *Pathinaru Vayathinile* end. Sridevi had to fill fairly large shoes, considering the role had been played by B. Saroja Devi (*Bhaaga Pirivinai*, Tamil, 1959) and Nutan (*Khandan*, Hindi, 1965) previously. But by now, she had become so adept at her craft that this didn't seem like much of a challenge.

Of these 11 Malayalam releases Sridevi had in 1977, *Oonjaal* had an interesting narrative. Literally meaning 'a swing', *Oonjaal* oscillates between obsessive love and extreme hatred. Rajan (M.G. Soman) grows up with deep loathing for his adoptive uncle though the reason for this is not quite clear. Even as a child, Rajan seethes with rage at the mention of his name and takes it out on his cousin Sumithra (Sridevi) who is the said uncle's daughter. The uncle sees red when he hears of Rajan's atrocities and unleashes unspeakable physical abuse on the boy. But this only makes Rajan angrier and he continues to pull hateful pranks on Sumithra. By the time Sumithra grows up, she is terrified of her cousin. Her father (veteran actor K.P. Ummer) wants to marry her off but every time a prospective groom visits, Rajan gatecrashes the party and wreaks havoc. By now he is obsessed with Sumithra and will not let any other man marry her. He declares that if she were to get married to anyone other than him, he would kill both of them. Only he was to make her his bride. Sumithra shivers in horror. The uncle does not tolerate it and manages to sneak in a prospective match, Madhu (Raghavan). Madhu and Sumithra like each other and their marriage is fixed. The uncle and Rajan keep roaring at each other—one challenges that he will see the wedding through, while the other dares him to try. At the centre of this feud is Sumithra, terrified—despite all assurances from relatives and friends—that Rajan is going to kill her. Sridevi portrays Sumithra's utter confusion and dread perfectly. Her agreement to the union with Madhu is not unequivocal (though she looks forward to married life) and her feelings about Rajan's love for her are ambivalent. The only thing she is sure of, is her fear of Rajan. The morning after her wedding, she wakes up in cold sweat having dreamt of Rajan breaking into her private quarters and trying to kill her groom. In the dream, for a brief moment before he goes in for the kill, Sumithra confesses that she has always loved Rajan but never reciprocated for fear of her father.

If there was one characteristic which distinguished Sridevi's time in the South Indian film industries (before she joined the Hindi film industry for good), it was that a majority of her roles were well-written and layered which gave her a lot to work with. *Oonjaal* is a great example of this. Despite giving her the stardom she deserved and craved, Bollywood never really offered her roles that would do justice to her acting muscles. Malayalam cinema also gave Sridevi her first known attempt at a double role. *Angeekaaram* had her playing a mother and daughter. A dying Sathi (Sridevi) instructs her daughter, Viji (also Sridevi), to find her estranged husband and convince him that she has never been unfaithful to him. Vijayan (Vincent) has left his old life behind and has built a new one with Malini (Prameela). Viji tracks them down and when Malini, Vijayan's current wife, is made aware of his past transgressions she is filled with anguish. Malini finds out that young Vijayan had a one-night stand with Sathi, and had reluctantly agreed to a court marriage before leaving for his palatial mansion in another town. Like all impressionable heroes of the 1970s, Vijayan had then been convinced of his wife's unfaithfulness by the scheming Ravi—his cousin who always had a thing for Sathi. She had been rejecting his advances and therefore, deserved to be punished. Vijayan 'saw' Sathi with another man and was immediately convinced of her infidelity. He promptly ditched her and proceeded to get married to his distant cousin, Malini. They spend a happy married life, with the exception of having a child. Now he refuses to accept the newfound daughter but Malini showers her with affection. Sridevi plays an elderly character for the first time as Sathi. Though she was just 14 years old, she had been working without a break for a decade. The experience showed. Through her performance, she deftly portrays the contrast between a teenage girl and her old mother.

Angeekaaram was the last time Sridevi and I.V. Sasi collaborated on a Malayalam film. After this they came together again in 1979 for *Pagalil Oru Iravu*, which was a frame-to-frame remake of *Aalinganam* in Tamil. In this movie, Vincent's and Raghavan's roles were played by Vijaykumar and Ravikumar respectively.

After this interesting spurt in Malayalam films during that one year, Sridevi didn't do a whole lot of movies in that language in the '70s. But some two decades later, she returned with what's possibly her most remembered film in Malayalam—*Devaraagam* (1996). By this time, Sridevi was a well-established institution in Bollywood. In fact her prime years in Hindi cinema were behind her and in just about a year, she would hang up her boots for a while. There was no reason for her to appear in a Malayalam film at this stage, that too directed by a non-mainstream filmmaker. The reason she did this goes back to the late 1960s when she was about to start working in the movies as a toddler. Before the movies she had worked in a few print ads, and the first one of them—a soap ad—was shot by a young aspiring filmmaker who was biding his time doing odd jobs. His name was Bharathan. Over the next five years, since the advertisement, Bharathan learned the ropes of filmmaking by assisting other directors. He broke into the scene with *Prayanam* (1975), which—along with some later films like *Thakara*—established him as the pioneer of a new kind of cinema in Malayalam. Bharathan also made a number of Tamil films including the landmark *Thevar Magan* (1992), which was later remade in Hindi as *Virasat* (1997). He seemed to get a kick out of hiring big stars for performance-oriented projects. It was nothing short of a casting coup to cast Sivaji Ganesan and Kamal Haasan together for *Thevar Magan*. And in a similar vein, casting Arvind Swamy and Sridevi for *Devaraagam* was quite a feat back in 1996.

Devaraagam had an unusual plot. Lakshmi (Sridevi)

has taken a fancy to the village priest's son, the handsome Vishnu (Arvind Swamy). He responds to her advances but his status as a celibate priest-to-be doesn't allow him to be in a relationship, so they end up marrying clandestinely. They consummate the marriage but decide to keep it a secret from everyone, at least for now. Soon, a wily relative of Lakshmi fixes a match for her and her father uses emotional manipulation to get her to marry the guy. And it is Vishnu, Lakshmi's secret husband, who has to officiate the wedding. After the marriage, she realizes she might be carrying Vishnu's child. The climax is rather unusual for a '90s film.

For a Sridevi fan, it might be hard to fathom the kind of heights she had already scaled before she came to Hindi cinema. Most observers would say she was only trying to find her bearings through her early Bollywood films. But the fact is, she had already 'found it' more than a decade before.

Fourteen

Devi Diva

'For the common Telugu audience, NTR was like a demi-God. They never thought of his age per se,' Telugu film journalist and critic Jalapathy told me over a call, as we chatted about Sridevi's Telugu films. Nandamuri Taraka Rama Rao or NTR was an imposing figure not only in Telugu cinema, but in India's national political arena as well. NTR started his movie career in the 1950s. This was around the time Raj Kapoor, Dilip Kumar and Dev Anand started making waves in the North; MGR and Sivaji Ganesan did so in Tamil Nadu; and Uttam Kumar did in Bengali cinema. Starting with 'everyman' roles, his work in mythological films became his mainstay. In fact, his depiction of Krishna, Karna and Duryodhana are considered pretty iconic in the annals of Telugu cinema. And like the gods he was playing on-screen, NTR was fast becoming divine himself.

The 1970s represented a transitional period in Indian cinema. The established stars had their time in the sun and age was catching up with them. But instead of making way for the new, most of them were holding fort. Dev Anand, Sivaji Ganesan, MGR, Uttam Kumar were all as active as ever and playing leading men. Their demi-god status in South India added to the durability of Tamil and Telugu superstars. And the fact that they were dancing around with heroines half their age didn't matter either. After all, she had played his granddaughter barely seven years ago in *Badi Panthulu* (1972). From granddaughter to heroine—has that ever happened before this? That's for film historians to answer. However, hitmaker K. Raghavendra Rao was convinced that the Sridevi–NTR combo would set the screen ablaze. And that is exactly what happened.

After *Vetagadu*'s success, the floodgates were open. In the next seven years, NTR and Sridevi appeared in 11 more films. *Vetagadu* was followed by *Aatagadu* and *Rowdy Ramudu Konte Krishnudu*. In the latter, NTR's son Nandamuri Balakrishna co-starred as his friend. Balakrishna emerged as a massively popular star in the late 1980s and '90s and continues to be frightfully popular. Social media is flooded with Balakrishna memes.

The second definitive Sridevi–NTR movie, *Sardar Papa Rayudu*, released in 1980. The hero was named and modelled after a legendary figure, a rebel bandit who fought the Mughals in the early eighteenth century. The eponymous hero was played by NTR himself, though in this case he fights the British. As India attains independence, his enemies frame him and he lands up in prison. His son, also NTR of course, grows up to be a cop. Sridevi plays his girlfriend.

In a number of early Telugu films, Sridevi played different versions of the shrew. She would start with a dislike of the hero, calling him names and indulging in one-upmanship on occasion. At this stage, she would wear jeans and shirts. Eventually, the hero's attempts to woo her would bear fruit and she would see the 'error of her ways' and fall in love with him. By this time, she would have switched to wearing saris. Her characters follow this template in most of her Telugu films, which became a blueprint for her early Bollywood films (mainly because these were remakes of their Telugu counterparts). These films were made with the sole intent of highlighting the hero's histrionics. It was more so with NTR because his over-the-top dialogue delivery, mannerisms and animated gesticulations were great crowd-pleasers. It didn't matter that he was 57, playing heroes in their 30s and serenading a heroine who was 40 years his junior. As Jalapathy mentioned to me, the Telugu audiences viewed NTR as a god gracing the screen with his presence. In this scenario, the heroine's primary job was to make the hero look good. Most such films did not offer Sridevi too many dialogues or scenes to sink her teeth into. But she had by then spent over a decade working with stalwarts from different states of India. She knew how to get noticed, how to get audiences to root for her and how to make them dance to her tune. And dance they did!

On the subject of age, many would cringe at the thought of men in their 50s romancing heroines half their age. In 1980 when *Sardar Papa Rayudu* hit the screens, Dev Anand (the same age as NTR) had two releases and one of them was directed by him. Even now, when I am writing this book the Khan trio of Bollywood—each of them as old as NTR was back then—make films with actresses much younger than them.

Sridevi had impeccable chemistry with these older stars; especially NTR, ANR and Krishna. Scan the comments on any NTR–Sridevi song on YouTube and you'll know. Anyhow, coming back to *Sardar Papa Rayudu*. The film was helmed by Dasari Narayana Rao, a filmmaker equally successful in both Hindi and Telugu cinema. Interestingly, as Jalapathy pointed out in our call, there was a distinction between how he and K. Raghavendra Rao handled a talent like Sridevi. He said: 'In K. Raghavendra Rao's films, she was more about the glamour. Whereas in the films directed by Dasari Narayana Rao, she got performance-oriented roles.' Dasari Narayana Rao was the one who directed Sridevi's first true-blue solo heroine film in Telugu, *Bangarakka* (1977), where she was paired opposite Murali Mohan. Dasari Narayana Rao also directed her in *Bobbili Puli* (1982), another blockbuster with NTR.

In *Bobbili Puli*, NTR's character is arrested after a manhunt and his former lover, played by Sridevi, is the prosecuting advocate. All eyes are on NTR as he enters the courtroom, draped in chains. After he has taken the oath, she asks him his name. 'Bobbili Puli (the tiger of Bobbili),' he slowly utters in his gruff voice. 'What is your *real* name?' she asks again. 'Bobbili Puli!' he repeats, agitated. She is equally agitated. They obviously have history. She reminds him that the last time he was in court he had identified himself as Major Chakradhar, a decorated war hero of the Indian Army. He tells her that the man, Chakradhar, is all but dead and that this was his only identity now. She asks about all the people he is accused of murdering. With great pride, he accepts that he killed them because they were enemies of the nation. Her voice wavers as she realizes that he will go to the gallows for this. She breaks down and sobs uncontrollably.

In this iconic scene from *Bobbili Puli*, NTR's character points out loopholes in the system which rewarded him for killing enemies at the border but is now punishing him for killing some enemies of the nation. As per the law of the land, Bobbili Puli is sentenced to death. As is obvious, the scenes were meant to highlight NTR's acting prowess.

With those gestures and that gravelly voice, he was quite a presence on the screen. However, Sridevi as the lawyer made her presence felt to such an extent that even diehard NTR fans cannot conceive of that movie without her in it. When she breaks down, you get her disappointment. You just get it. After *Bobbili Puli* if one were to watch *Zakhmi Sher* (1984), the official Bollywood remake directed by Dasari Narayana Rao himself, you'd sorely miss Sridevi's antics.

In *Justice Chowdary* (1982), the trio of K. Raghavendra Rao, Sridevi and NTR teamed up for the last time. Before this, three films of note—*Gaja Donga*, *Kondaveeti Simham* and *Satyam Shivam*—came out in 1981. *Kondaveeti Simham* was loosely based on the Tamil film *Thanga Pathakkam* (1974). This Tamil film inspired a slew of remakes in Telugu and Hindi in the '80s, including *Farz Aur Kanoon* and *Shakti* (both 1982). *Kondaveeti Simham* focussed on the clash between a son and his father, who is a righteous police officer (NTR). Unbeknownst to everyone, the officer has an elder son, Ramu (also NTR). Sridevi plays Ramu's girlfriend. Here again was a film designed to showcase NTR's theatrics, but Sridevi managed to get noticed. In the climax, as NTR spouts a long pre-death monologue, the focus is on the heroes. However, Sridevi features prominently in the scene. In fact, the camera keeps panning to her face as she sheds copious tears.

Justice Chowdary showed that she had attained the maturity to shoulder a mainstream heroine role. The dance numbers were showing flashes of the magic her Bollywood fans would worship her for. There are dramatic scenes with NTR where she spars with him, neck and neck. Unlike *Bobbili Puli*, here she has long lines of dialogue that allow her to go toe-to-toe with the veteran actor.

Satyam Shivam was K. Raghavendra Rao's re-imagination

of Manmohan Desai's *Suhaag* (1979). NTR reprised Amitabh Bachchan's role, while Shashi Kapoor's role in the original was reproduced by another superstar of Telugu cinema—ANR.

By the '70s, ANR already had a good two decades behind him with iconic roles like *Devadasu* (1953) and *Bhakt Tukaram* (1971) in which Sridevi played his daughter. His first film with her as a heroine was *Muddala Koduku*. They ended up doing seven films as a lead pair (though they shared screen space in three more films, Krishna and NTR were her heroes there). Though this might seem like a small number, Sridevi and ANR were part of a film which created box-office history in Telugu cinema.

At the time of writing this book (2020), *Dangal* and *Baahubali* were two of the most successful movies in the history of Indian cinema (or that's what we're told). But while the box-office figures are easy to get, figures about how many weeks these films ran in theatres aren't as easily accessible. And maybe there is a reason for this. None of these films would've run for more than 10–12 weeks, regardless of the mammoth box-office collections. That's three months tops. *Baahubali* is a Telugu film. One of Telugu cinema's most commercially successful movies was *Premabhishekam* (1981). Although it's difficult to quote actual box-office numbers, the film ran for around 533 days. That's more than a whole year! The film created a history of sorts.

Jalapathy said:

Sridevi did one of the most landmark Telugu films with ANR: *Premabhishekam*. It ran almost for a year. The plot is very similar to *Kal Ho Na Ho* (2003). ANR is a terminally ill cancer patient who is in love with Sridevi. But he doesn't want to tell her about it, so he pretends to be in love with another girl (Jayasudha). It was just a reason to break up with her. This itself was unique for the time, and the film was also a musical hit...all the songs were superhit. After NTR and Sridevi, this film established ANR and Sridevi as a hit pair. And Sridevi was one of the reasons for its success.

Directed by hitmaker Dasari Narayana Rao, the film struck a chord with the audiences. There was a tinge of the fatalist *Devadasu* persona which that generation had grown up watching ANR play. But the character didn't wallow in misery. The first half of the film has ANR and Sridevi doing the lets-groove-in-the-gardens routine. And Sridevi hits it out of the park. If fans look closely at the dance numbers, beyond the obvious age disparity, they will notice Sridevi constantly matching her pace with veterans like NTR and ANR. It was a different pace and beat when she was with good dancers like Chiranjeevi, Kamal Haasan and Jeetendra. The best of them would strive to be at the top of their game to keep up with her. But with the veterans, she seemed to slow down a bit so that even with them she seemed completely in sync. After *Premabhishekam*, people couldn't get enough of ANR and Sridevi and *Bangaru Kanuka* (1982) reaped the benefits. Once again, Sridevi played a woman wiser than her years. In this period, whether in Hindi or Telugu cinema every heroine had only one objective: to get married to the hero. The heroine would do a good chunk of dancing, a bit of fooling around and a bout of crying. But in *Bangaru Kanuka*, Roopa (Sridevi) sacrifices her love life at the altar of family responsibilities when her brother dies leaving his three little kids with her. This was a film where along with all the prancing around that mainstream cinema required her to do, there were some intense scenes where she could emote and lock horns with an old-timer like

ANR. Another hit around this time was *Sri Ranga Neethulu* (1983), which had shades of *Bombai Ka Babu* (1960) and *Zameer* (1975) inasmuch as the protagonist impersonates someone and then falls in love with that someone's sibling. Though *Sri Ranga Neethulu* is a very different film from the ones mentioned above, Sridevi does end up impersonating Vijayashanthi's character and then falls for ANR's character (Vijayashanthi's stepbrother). Go figure. But the film did work and the songs were a rage.

When it comes to the star system in Indian cinema, one always tends to think in threes. In Hindi, we've had the triumvirate of Dev Anand, Dilip Kumar and Raj Kapoor; and eventually the Great Khans in the '90s. In Tamil cinema, the holy trinity of Sivaji Ganesan, Gemini Ganesan and MGR ruled the space for decades only to be taken over by Rajinikanth, Kamal Haasan and Mohan in the '80s. However, this theory of trinity doesn't hold up as one tries to wrap one's head around the history of Telugu cinema.

Jalapathy helped decode it for me over our interview: 'Both NTR and ANR were the pillars of Telugu movie industry. They were our first superstars. In the second generation, Krishna and Sobhan Babu were the two major superstars. And coming to the third generation, Chiranjeevi, Balakrishna, Nagarjuna and Venkatesh were the stars who ruled the roost.'

The entire superstar hegemony in Indian cinema has always been overwhelmingly male dominated. It still is, as much as it is made to appear otherwise. Women were not considered capable of headlining casts of mainstream cinemas. And yet, there have been women since the early days of Indian cinema who clawed their way in and made a massive impact. Women like Nargis, Sitara Devi, Savitri, Jayalalithaa, Jaya Prada, Jayasudha and, of course, Sridevi.

Sridevi managed to consistently draw attention to herself
no matter who her male co-actor was. This was despite many
of these actors being, quite literally, worshipped by their
fans. And all these films were written and directed in ways
that highlighted the man. The hero. The heroine was little
more than arm candy, meant to establish the hero as the
ultimate object of desire. Sridevi's triumph in these overtly
male-dominated film industries was that she could, with
little support from the script or the plot, force everyone
to take note of her. If you were to talk to any of the NTR,
ANR, Kamal or Rajinikanth fans from the 1970s and '80s,
most of them will not be hard-pressed to recall the roles
she played opposite these actors.

Sridevi's Telugu work is also a testament to some of
the directors she was working with. K. Raghavendra Rao
of course was the most frequent collaborator. They worked
together in 16 films, and I am not even including the Hindi
films they teamed up for. Unlike most filmmakers of his
time, Raghavendra Rao had perfected the art of projecting
a heroine in those days of glitter and bling. And within a
commercial format, he managed to incorporate scenes for
the heroines that would allow them to sink their teeth into
their characters. Case in point: *Devatha* (1982).

Devatha was about two sisters in love with the same
man. Simple enough. Sobhan Babu played this much-
desired man, while Sridevi and Jaya Prada were the sisters.
One sister had to sacrifice, obviously. About one scene in
the movie, Raghavendra Rao explained in the TV show
Soundaryalahari, on which he featured with Sridevi and
Ram Gopal Varma:

> Two girls falling in love with one boy is not an
> uncommon idea. I kept thinking about it. In the scene

where she admits she loves the boy her sister is also (secretly) in love with, the audience knows this fact. I wanted to add some gimmick. The scene was written normally, but could we add something to it to make it a little more interesting? I thought about it for a few days and then got this idea.[33]

In the aforementioned scene, the two sisters want to reveal to each other that they are in love. But who'll go first? After a lot of false starts, the sisters decide to toss a coin. They toss a coin but it gets stuck in the ceiling. All this while, anticipation has been building in the audience that knows these girls are in love with the same guy. The audience also knows that the one to speak first will get the man, because the other sister will choose to sacrifice her love. Sridevi suggests Jaya Prada, being the elder of the two should be the one to start. To make the confession easier, as one of them speaks the other keeps her eyes shut. Excitement is wrought on their faces, and Sridevi is still smiling as she shuts her eyes. She jumps with joy as her sister says she plans to get married. Jaya Prada reveals it's Ram Babu (Shobhan Babu) she is in love with. The camera swings to Sridevi's face and in precisely the number of seconds it takes to register a change of expression, her smile disappears. She is distressed, but her eyes are still shut. Jaya Prada goes on about Ram Babu and how she can barely conceive of a life without him. When it is Sridevi's turn to speak, she opens her eyes and while staring at her sister's face cooks up a story about bagging a new job at her college.

---

[33]'Soundaryalahari–సౌందర్యయలహరి–2nd November 2014', YouTube, https://tinyurl.com/y864ms2v. Accessed on 29 May 2023.

Raghavendra Rao said in the show:

> When the idea of this scene struck me, I worked it out in
> reverse order. Whether to add it or not wasn't decided
> at the outset. Some scenes become more interesting
> if you delay them. You talk to your actors, let them
> think about it. They have to time their movements
> and reactions accordingly. Every shot was meticulously
> planned and calculated. I was very satisfied with this
> scene, how it turned out.[34]

Rao's conception of the scene and the performances, especially
Sridevi's, elevates a stock scene of 1980s mainstream cinema to
a whole different level. *Devatha* had Sridevi star with Sobhan
Babu and Mohan Babu, alongside Jaya Prada. Jalapathy
explains, 'It was one of the milestones in Sridevi's career in
Telugu cinema. The film featured a song called "Velluvachi
Godaramma", which became a trendsetter in filming love
songs, particularly in Telugu cinema. Raghavendra Rao used
the same technique in Hindi also.'

What Jalapathy was explaining to me was K. Raghavendra
Rao's elaborate set-up of props, such as utensils, saris and
fruits to shoot songs. As ludicrous as it may seem now, this
approach changed the way 'love songs' were being mounted
in big-ticket Telugu and Hindi films. Rao earlier employed
this device in the song 'Mogga Puindelanade' from *Ooruki
Monagadu* (1981), which had a second life in *Himmatwala*
as 'Nainon Mein Sapna'.

With Sobhan Babu she had earlier worked as a child
in the film *Naa Thammudu* (1971), where she survived a
near-fatal accident we have discussed earlier in the book.

---

[34]Ibid.

They went on to work together in a dozen-odd films, out of which *Devatha* and *Karthika Deepam* (1979) are noteworthy. *Devatha* was remade in Hindi as *Tohfa* with Sridevi and Jaya Prada reprising their roles. In Telugu films—with the aid of directors like K. Raghavendra Rao, Dasari Narayana Rao and A. Kodandarami Reddy—Sridevi's roles were mounted with a lot of bling. She oozed glamour and charisma in the songs, but she was also (often in the same film) offered plenty of leg room to stretch her acting muscles.

In an industry filled with competent heroines like Jaya Prada and Jayasudha, Sridevi was the one to get roles where she could showcase her histrionics. She was the 'other' woman. She was the one sacrificing her love. She was the one who laid down her life in the end. Much like in *Devatha*, in *Karthika Deepam* Sridevi plays the woman who chooses to give up her claim for her man. The hero (Sobhan Babu) rescues her from a brothel and, as inevitably as the Laws of Motion, the two are drawn to each other. An environmental disaster separates them, giving him reason to believe that she's dead. Years later, when he has moved on and raised a new family, she comes back into his life. The film earned equal attention from the box-office as well as the critics, and Sridevi's performance was greatly appreciated. Jalapathy goes so far as to say, 'That was one film in her career which was a testament to her acting skills.'

She couldn't help but act. It was in her very bones now. In the present era, where every creative endeavour is taken apart, analysed and discussed, it is difficult to imagine a young actor who couldn't explain what she did and how she did it. And yet Sridevi did just that. If YouTubers existed back then and if one of them were to pose a question to her about 'craft', she would have nothing to say. Nothing at all.

Fifteen

The Last Leg

In a career encompassing 300 films, Sridevi worked with a number of male stars in various languages. But if we were to talk about her most frequent co-star ever, one name would emerge. That is Telugu superstar Ghattamaneni Siva Rama Krishna Murthy, more popularly known as Krishna, with whom she did iconic films like *Maa Nanna Nirdoshi* and *Vidhi Vilasam* (both in 1970). As a heroine she did around 31 films with Krishna. He was so impossibly busy in those days that, as Jalapathy tells me, some directors actually shot footage of him sleeping for later use in their films. With *Burripalem Bullodu* (1979), Sridevi became Krishna's heroine. It was the first time they were paired as an on-screen couple. But it was a year later with *Gharana Donga*, that Krishna and Sridevi became a team that Telugu audiences wanted to see again and again. It was one of the three films where Sridevi, Krishna and K. Raghavendra Rao collaborated; the other two being *Adavi Simhalu* (1983) and *Vajrayudham* (1985). All three were immensely successful movies. *Gharana Donga* also pitted Sridevi against both Krishna and Mohan Babu. It was a 1980 film and Sridevi was still three years away from ruling the national film scene. However, the likes of the song 'O Muddu Krishna' prove that she had already found her 'mojo'. She was ready to take on anyone. In a span of 35 movies over 18 years, Krishna and Sridevi not only played lovers and spouses but also played each other's parents. Yes, parents. While Sridevi played Krishna's daughter in *Maa Nanna Nirdoshi*, he played her son in *Samajaniki Saval* (1979). *Guru Shishyulu* (1981) was another money-spinner at the box-office. It featured Krishna and ANR together with Sridevi.

Ram Robert Rahim (1980) was the remake of *Amar Akbar Anthony* with Krishna playing Robert Gonsalves (Krishna's answer to Amitabh Bachchan's Anthony). Sridevi reprised Parveen Babi's Jenny from the original, called Jenny here as well. Rajinikanth played Inspector Ram, an echo of Vinod Khanna's Amar; while Akbar Illahabadi became Rahim, played by Chandra Mohan. This was the same Chandra Mohan who was Sridevi's principal co-star from *Padaharella Vayasu*. This was a bit of a casting coup, back in the day.

Krishnavataram (1982) was a great success, and so was *Mundadugu* (1983). By this time, Sridevi had made successful inroads into Bollywood and for a while her Hindi and Telugu films were feeding off each other. For three years following *Himmatwala* (1983), she did around 16 films which were remakes of Telugu and Tamil hits. These were often directed by the same filmmakers and they often starred her in the lead. *Sultanat, Bhagwaan Dada, Karma* and *Nagina* (all 1986) were Sridevi's first set of Hindi films which were not remakes. Meanwhile in Telugu, the Sridevi–Krishna rampage continued through films like *Ramarajyamlo Bheemaraju, Adavi Simhalu* (remade in Hindi as *Jaani Dost* and *Pachani Kapuram*). The last one was a roaringly successful entertainer, inspired from *Pyar Jhukta Nahin* (1985). This in turn got inspiration from a Pakistani film called *Aina* (1977), which was copied from *Aa Gale Lag Jaa* (1973). You get the drift.

Khaidi Rudrayya was the last collaboration of Sridevi and A. Kodandarami Reddy, a very important director as far as her Telugu career is concerned. She had done seven films with him, four of which were with Krishna as her co-star. *Khaidi Rudrayya* was the last film of this trio.

The late '80s was the time when action was the only genre that could cause some flutter at the box-office. This trend was prominent in both Telugu as well as Hindi cinema, which consistently churned out film after film with 'tough' protagonists who seemed to like getting into a tussle every now and then. Fight scenes were like the item numbers of today. These heroes would brood throughout the film, looking as if nothing could ever make them smile, except in songs where they'd gleefully prance about the green. *Khaidi Rudrayya* was a film that fell squarely in the middle of this category. In these films, most heroines were present only in songs. They were lucky if they got one or two proper scenes to showcase their acting chops. But Sridevi was not most heroines. She was in a league of her own, not really in competition with anyone (as a close examination of this book will prove). She was an electrifying presence throughout the film and when it was remade in Hindi as *Waqt Ki Awaz*, she made an equally strong impression there (if not more).

By this time, Sridevi had established herself as a major force in mainstream Bollywood and she was now a bit picky about her projects in the South. Between 1985 and 1988, she was working almost exclusively with Krishna in Telugu cinema with just one exception—a collaboration with Kamal Haasan called *Oka Radha Iddaru Krishnulu* (which was an adaptation of the eponymous book by Yandamuri Veerendranath). This was Kamal and Sridevi's second collaboration in Telugu, the first one being Balachander's *Aakali Rajyam* (the Telugu version of *Varumayin Niram Sivappu*). It was also their last film together.

Sridevi appeared with Krishna one last time in *Maharajasree Mayagadu*. The year was 1988. After this, she did five Telugu films with the next generation of actors.

∽

It was the late 1980s. Director K. Raghavendra Rao was in his car, pondering over his next project. Also travelling with him was the writer Srinivas Chakravarthi, who had written a number of popular Telugu films. Srinivas had a brainwave. He had an idea that he was toying with, a story about a goddess falling in love with a man. Raghavendra Rao lapped up the idea. It was, in fact, ideal for what was in his mind for some time. He had presented Sridevi in all her hues: as a traditional middle-class girl, as a rustic woman, a city-bred upwardly-mobile girl, but this was his chance to show her as she was—a veritable goddess. A series of discussions on the story and script followed. Raghavendra Rao had sit-ins with Yandamuri Veerendranath and Jandhyala, who co-wrote the screenplay.[35]

This was how the idea of *Jagadeka Veerudu Athiloka Sundari* (1990) was born.

The plot was rather simple. Indraja, Lord Indra's daughter, descends to Earth and misplaces her ring. The ring is important and she can't be back in heaven without it. It ends up in the hands of Raju, a tour guide (where else have we heard of a tour guide called Raju before?). Indraja and Raju cross paths, of course; and they fall in love,

---

[35]Vijaya Mary, S.B., 'Celebrating 30 Years of the Chiranjeevi–Sridevi Telugu Blockbuster "Jagadeka Veerudu Athiloka Sundari"', *The Hindu*, 9 May 2020, https://tinyurl.com/2p8tcreh. Accessed on 8 June 2023.

of course. Till now, there were two films which had Sridevi and Chiranjeevi share screen-space: *Mosagadu* (1980) and *Rani Kasula Rangamma* (1981). In the first, he was a villain. The second film was an out-and-out Sridevi star vehicle in which he plays a spoilt brat, who eventually turns over a new leaf. The opening credits are entirely composed of Sridevi stills from the film. But by the time *Jagadeka Veerudu Athiloka Sundari* came along, Chiranjeevi was a major star in the Telugu constellation. Jalapathy told me in an interview:

Jagadeka Veerudu Athiloka Sundari is still considered one of the classics of Telugu cinema. Let me tell you a story about it. Sridevi played an angel or *apsara* in the film. Chiranjeevi was at the peak of his career during 1989–90. He was giving continuous, back-to-back hits, and he had become a megastar. And Sridevi was the number one star in Bollywood at the same time. So, Raghavendra Rao decided to bring these two together—the biggest star of Telugu cinema and the biggest star of Bollywood—for one film. He knew he could attract a huge audience if he could get these two megastars together. And he decided to depict her as an angel. If you watch the film *Jagadeka Veerudu Athiloka Sundari*, she looks like a goddess. The film begins with Chiranjeevi but the moment Sridevi appears, she is shown coming down from heaven to the Himalayas. She was made to look like a goddess. So the film ran more because of Sridevi, rather than Chiranjeevi. This was the first time in Telugu cinema that a film having a number one male star, ran because of the female star. And because of the music of Ilaiyaraaja. It was a sensational musical hit. Even today people hum the songs.

In an article in *The Hindu* celebrating the thirtieth anniversary of *Jagadeka Veerudu Athiloka Sundari*, journalist S.B. Vijaya Mary related a story about the film's release and its impact:

> It was a stormy night on May 9, 1990. The unified state of Andhra Pradesh was being lashed by heavy rains. There was a power cut as producer Ashwini Dutt sat for dinner with his family—wife, three children and his father—in the dark. There was a storm brewing inside him as well. His most ambitious film *Jagadeka Veerudu Athiloka Sundari* had released that morning but most roads and theatres were flooded and the Howrah Express that was carrying the film prints to Vijayawada had got stuck midway as the rail tracks got washed away. 'Will this be my last film?' he wondered, feeling utterly dejected.
>
> Defying the adversity, the socio-fantasy film went on to become a blockbuster hit and one of the biggest successes for Ashwini Dutt.[36]

On the TV show *Soundaryalahari*, Sridevi, K. Raghavendra Rao and RGV came together to talk about their movies. Among the films discussed was *Jagadeka Veerudu Athiloka Sundari*. Sridevi explained how her look in the film was achieved:

> At the very outset, Raghavendra Garu showed me a sketch of how the apsara should look like. He always shared every such detail before the film started. He had a vision for them, like how a heroine should be. For example, in *Vetagadu*, *Devatha*, *Tohfa* etc. But this is especially true of this movie. He worked a lot in *Jagadeka Veerudu Athiloka Sundari*. Later Neeta Lulla and Manish

---

[36]Ibid.

Malhotra were called in from Bombay. Neeta Lulla did the dresses. I remember, a green dress became very famous. Later it was mostly used by changing colours. But I felt really good in it.[37]

Jagadeka Veerudu Athiloka Sundari was one of Neeta Lulla's earliest works as a designer in films. She was also working with Sridevi on Yash Chopra's *Chandni* around the same time. She had an assistant, who went by the name Manish Malhotra. In April 2018, Manish paid a tribute to Sridevi on the pages of *Vogue India*. There he describes his first experience of meeting her:

> I must have been in college when I first watched *Himmatwala* (1983), and I was instantly enamoured. Be it those twinkling eyes or her poise, I loved everything about Sridevi. I finally met her a few years later, when Rakesh Shrestha, legendary photographer of the time, introduced us. I remember waiting anxiously at Mumbai's Mehboob Studio as she wrapped up a song sequence in a striking red Amrapali costume alongside Vinod Khanna.[38]

The song he talks about could only have been 'Baandh Lo Ghungroo, Naacho Sanam' from Shomu Mukherjee's *Pathar Ke Insan* (1990). Manish also said:

> I saw her next when she asked to meet me at the Centaur Hotel—she wanted me to design a sweater for her role in *Khuda Gawah* (1992) and style a song

[37]'Soundaryalahari–సౌందర్యలహరి–2nd November 2014', YouTube, https://tinyurl.com/y864ms2v. Accessed on 29 May 2023.
[38]Malhotra, Manish, '"Sridevi Will Forever Be, Boney Ji, Janhvi and Khushi's Best Friend"', *Vogue*, 12 April 2018, https://tinyurl.com/2mveb2yk. Accessed on 23 May 2023.

in *Aadmi Aur Apsara* (1991). Before I knew it, I, all of
23, was on a flight to Chennai carrying two black and
gold jackets, for her and Chiranjeevi Sir.[39]

The second film he talked about, *Aadmi aur Apsara*, was the
Hindi dubbed version of *Jagadeka Veerudu Athiloka Sundari*.
Before this in 2009, Manish gave an interview to *Times of
India* where he said: 'I remember the time when I had
to bring a set of costumes to Chennai for Sridevi and
Chiranjeevi for the movie *Jagadeka Veerudu Athiloka Sundari*.
Sridevi specifically wanted two black dresses for a song
they were shooting.'[40]

The song was 'Yamaho Nee Yama Yama Andham'. The
film was a high-water mark for Telugu mainstream films
of the time and was one of Sridevi's biggest successes in
Telugu.

RGV met Sridevi on the sets of *Aakhari Poratam*. He has
always professed himself to be the greatest fan of Sridevi
on the planet. His film *Mast* was an ode to her. But he first
got to see her in the flesh during the shooting of the song
'Tella Cheeraku' from *Aakhari Poratam*. Around this time he
was planning to make his first film, *Siva*, which put him on
the map. He had brought the idea to Nagarjuna, who was
seriously considering starring in it. Nagarjuna was Sridevi's
co-star in *Aakhari Poratam*, K. Raghavendra Rao's fifteenth
Telugu film with Sridevi. It was also the first time she was
collaborating with Nagarjuna.

Nagarjuna was the son of ANR, with whom she had done
some of her most successful Telugu films. She had appeared
with ANR in their last film together, *S.P. Bhayankar*, just

---

[39]Ibid.
[40]'Tailored to Perfection: Manish Malhotra', *Times of India*, 5 August 2009,
https://tinyurl.com/45d4y9cw. Accessed on 29 May 2023.

four years prior to this. Nagarjuna had debuted two years before and had already done eight films, one of them with K. Raghavendra Rao. This was the first time he and Sridevi were cast opposite each other. They went on to work in three more films, two of them in Hindi: *Khuda Gawah* and *Mr Bechara*.

Sridevi played a hard-as-nails CBI officer Pravallika in *Aakhari Poratam*. In the movie, she's been chasing a ne'er-do-good evil baba who goes by the name Anantananda Swamy (Amrish Puri, speaking heavily accented Telugu). Under the garb of religious activities, the man indulges in all sorts of illegal tomfoolery that the '80s villains loved wallowing in including: extortion, smuggling and terrorism. Anantananda Swamy maintains his own army. He is planning an attack on Ravindra Kalakshetra ('turn the Kalakshetra into Kurukshetra,' says Anantananda to his minions), and it is up to Pravallika to foil his plans. She goes undercover as a performer and on the day of the attack, the-CBI-officer-turned-dancer prances on the stage with Vihari (Nagarjuna) with a plethora of apples for company. Mid-performance the chief guest is shot and Pravallika swings into action, gun akimbo.

The rest of the plot focusses on how she, with abundant help from Vihari, proceeds to demolish the Swamy's empire. Love blooms along the way but owing to a series of misunderstandings caused by Pravallika herself, Vihari falls for a different girl (Suhasini Maniratnam). In the final confrontation with Anantananda, officer Pravallika lays down her life.

Unlike most mainstream Telugu (or Hindi) films those days, Sridevi plays the principal action hero here with the 'hero' playing second fiddle. She not only fights the villain till the end, but dies with a lot of flourish—flashing a thumbs-up to Nagarjuna's character before breathing her last.

Raghavendra Rao says in an episode of the show *Soundaryalahari*: 'She shows a thumbs-up signal before dying. Like "we won!" We had so many meetings to make sure the audience doesn't come away disappointed. Sridevi was dying on screen, after all. So, we used some images from the film, where the hero has flashbacks about her before ending the film.'[41]

Aakhari Poratam was a runaway hit, one of the most significant movies for Nagarjuna in that phase of his career. Sridevi was at the peak of her game, and she drove the crowds crazy despite the break in form. Telugu cinema, traditionally was all about the men displaying their machismo and roughing up bad guys. And obviously, the heroine doesn't die flashing a thumbs-up. But she did and the audience was lapping it up. By the way, there was a James Cameron film that came out a good three years after *Aakhari Poratam* where the hero (Arnold Schwarzenegger) goes down flashing the thumbs-up sign. Hmmm...well.

Coming back to RGV, the first instance that he had a proper interaction with his Goddess Sridevi was after *Siva* released. While he was doing the rounds of Nagarjuna's office trying to get *Siva* off the ground, he used to look at her house (which happened to fall on the way) from a distance and wonder how it managed to contain her. He says in his book *Guns and Thighs: The Story of my Life*:

> My journey to Sridevi started when I was preparing for
> my debut film *Siva*. I used to walk from Nagarjuna's office
> in Chennai to a neighbouring street where Sridevi used
> to live, and I would just stand and stare at her house. I

---

[41]'Soundaryalahari–సొందర్యలహరి–9th November 2014', YouTube, https://tinyurl.com/nhdhj8fw. Accesssed on 29 May 2023.

just couldn't believe that the goddess of beauty lived in
that stupid-looking house. I say stupid because I believed
that no brick-and-mortar house deserved to hold that
ethereal beauty called SRIDEVI. I used to desperately
hope to catch a glimpse of her as she went in or out
of her house, but sadly no such thing ever happened.[42]

If someone was to tell him then that she was going to
materialize right in front of him barely a few months later,
he probably would have laughed and moved on. But that
is how everything did pan out eventually. *Siva* released to
a thumping success (both the Telugu and Hindi versions,
might I add). A successful producer and cinematographer
in Telugu movies, S. Gopal Reddy, asked RGV if he would
like to make a movie with Sridevi. He said, and I quote:
'Are you mad or what? I will die just to see her, let alone
make a film with her!'[43]

Reddy fixed an appointment and took RGV to meet her.
He was stepping into the same building he used to ogle at
just a few months back. It was the early hours of the evening,
and one could imagine his elation when it turned out to be
a candlelight meeting. Powercuts weren't uncommon those
days, but who would expect the lights to go out right when
you are meeting the woman of your dreams?

Sridevi was packing for a flight to Mumbai so she
was moving from one corner of the room to the other
and from one room to the next, picking up knick-knacks
so as not to miss anything. She seemed to be in a rush.
Her fan sitting there was observing her every move with
deep awe and admiration. He was a fan, but he was also

---

[42]Varma, Ram Gopal, *Guns and Thighs: The Story of My Life*, Rupa Publications,
Delhi, 15 December 2015.
[43]Ibid.

a director. 'Every time she appeared and disappeared in a flash, the director in me started slow motioning her and running her backward and forward for my visual pleasure,' RGV says in his book. Sridevi said that she would like to work with a filmmaker like Ram Gopal Varma and went to catch her flight. RGV 'continued talking to her mother with enormous respect and awe because she had actually given birth to Sridevi'.[44]

RGV was walking on the clouds. It was in that delirious stupor that he wrote *Kshana Kshanam* which, by his own admission, he wrote 'with the one and only purpose of impressing Sridevi'.[45] *Kshana Kshanam* was a heist adventure, sort of an Indian *Romancing the Stone* sans the map and the hidden treasure. (Well, there's treasure.) A gang of hoodlums led by Paresh Rawal loot ₹1 crore from a bank vault. One of the robbers gets greedy and hides the loot in a place only he knows about, hoping to retrieve it later. And just to make the script more interesting, he slips the whereabouts in an envelope and stashes it in his brother's photo studio. The brother mistakenly hands over the envelope to Sridevi, who thinks she is just taking delivery of some passport photos she wanted developed from the studio. Paresh wants his money back and he chases her. Sridevi is on the run and into the mix comes Venkatesh, a small-time conman who's been posing as a cop. What ensues is one of the most fun, delightful adventure films in Indian cinema. It's refreshing, fast-paced, technically slick, filled with some great music (M.M. Keeravani) and is refreshingly different from most mainstream action films those days. Sridevi was an utter delight to watch. She was

---

[44]Ibid.
[45]Ibid.

in her element. The fun, effervescent girl of *Mr India* or *ChaalBaaz* can be seen in a similar avatar here. If you watch this film today on YouTube (or that jungle called OTT), you cannot take your eyes off her.

RGV had a similar experience even while directing that film. While shooting the song 'Andanantha Ettha Tara Theeram', RGV was pleased on the first take. But Master Sundaram, the choreographer, asked for one more take. RGV asked, 'Sir, why one more?' Sundaram took one more shot nevertheless, and again RGV liked it. But Master Sundaram was not happy and asked for another one. RGV pulled his assistant director to one side and asked what the problem was. He told RGV, 'Sir, you are looking at Sridevi Gaaru, but the dance master is looking at Venkatesh Gaaru!' That's when it dawned on him. All this while he was just staring at Sridevi. And you can't blame him.[46]

Through this film, Sridevi effortlessly slid into the '90s. From the garish makeup of the '80s through to the no-makeup look of *Kshana Kshanam*, she had managed to retain that quality of drawing attention to herself no matter what was happening in the frame.

Six years later, RGV repackaged the basic plot of *Kshana Kshanam* and tossed it at the Bollywood film audiences as *Daud*. But it wasn't the same film and the audiences chose to look the other way.

---

[46]'Soundaryalahari–సౌందర్యలహరి–9th November 2014', YouTube, https://tinyurl.com/nhdhj8fw. Accesssed on 29 May 2023.

Sixteen

All Good Things

One director who finds repeated mention in this book is S.P. Muthuraman. His directorial debut featured Sridevi as a child artist and they went on to work together in six films, many of them noteworthy and significant. Muthuraman is unarguably one of the most popular and iconic filmmakers of Tamil cinema. The 1980s started with him, Rajinikanth and Sridevi collaborating in two tentpole films. Both were multi-starrers but only one of them made a dent at the box-office.

Ranuva Veeran featured both Rajinikanth and Chiranjeevi along with Sridevi. Rajinikanth and Sridevi were already big stars in Tamil films and Chiranjeevi was consolidating his position in Telugu cinema. *Ranuva Veeran* was one of only two Tamil films in which Chiranjeevi featured in major roles. In both films, he played negative characters. Due to his presence, the film was also released in Telugu as *Bandipotu Simham*. The film is known for an arresting action sequence between the two men in the climax. But as usual—even in a movie full of grunting, sweating men making Karate poses and snapping at each other—Sridevi captures your attention and holds it. Among other highlights there is one rather interesting song sequence where Rajinikanth and Sridevi dance around between life-sized bottles of liquor, with a giant VAT-69 having pride of place. The song itself ('Malligai Poo') is an acquired taste. It was created by M.S. Vishwanathan, the illustrious composer.

But the film did not work at all and is one of the rare flops of the Rajinikanth–Sridevi team. The very next year, Muthuraman came up with another film featuring this awesome twosome. This was one of their most iconic Tamil films of all time: *Pokkiri Raja*. The plot was a repackaging of the Telugu superhit *Chuttalunnaru Jagratha*, starring Sridevi along with Krishna. This is one of the instances where the same film was made in three languages, and all of them had Sridevi in the lead. The Hindi version *Mawaali* was also a thumping success. The wafer-thin plot was about a man losing his job and being wrongfully convicted for a crime, mainly because his doppelgänger would crop up at the wrong place at the wrong time. Our hero bumps into his double in jail, and they join forces to clear his name. Sridevi plays the arm candy but she does get some opportunities to put her histrionics on display. And the Rajinikanth–Sridevi chemistry is undeniable. Sparks fly in the early scenes with banter between the two, before they actually become a couple.

The interesting thing about most of these movies, which were eventually remade frame by frame in Hindi, is that somehow the Hindi versions seem pale, caricaturish and pedestrian in comparison to the originals. This is especially acute in a film like *Pokkiri Raja* when you place it alongside *Mawaali*. The Tamil version is just as over the top, loud and in-your-face, but revisiting *Mawaali* today after seeing the original will make it seem devoid of any redeeming qualities.

If *Pokkiri Raja* was predictable, *Thanikattu Raja* was a

more wholesome offering with plenty for the actors to bite into. Rajinikanth plays a rebellious man who can't stand injustice, especially that meted out by the affluent class on the downtrodden. In a bid to save his lady love (Sridevi, who else?), he ends up killing a lecher. She realizes that the only way to save him from hanging for the crime is to give in to the advances of the wily Ehiraj (Jaishankar), who is rich and connected enough to cancel the death sentence and who wants nothing more than to marry her. When Rajinikanth is out of jail, he finds it difficult to be in a world where the love of his life has married someone else. But there's still unfinished business, scores to be settled. And Sridevi has to make the ultimate sacrifice. Compared to most of its contemporaries, *Thanikattu Raja* had a slightly more layered plot but the audience didn't respond to it at all.

Adutha Varisu, Sridevi's last film with S.P. Muthuraman, was a reworking of Mohan Sehgal's Hindi film *Raja Jani* (which in turn was based on the Hollywood film, *Anastasia*) and didn't have anything new to offer. In the movie, an heiress of a royal family has been missing for many years. Rajinikanth plays a hustler who finds a gypsy girl (Sridevi) and trains her to take the princess's place. But there are some slimy members of the clan who'd prefer that the heiress was dead. Eventually, it is discovered that she indeed *is* the real heiress who was kidnapped as a child. (Yawn.) There are some glittering musical pieces which allow Sridevi and Rajinikanth to shimmer and do their thing on the dance floor and around trees. Other than that, there's nothing else to drive home here.

Her last Tamil film was *Naan Adimai Illai* (1986), till she came back for the Tamil version of *English Vinglish* and a fantasy spectacle called *Puli* in 2015. *Naan Adimai Illai* was a remake of *Pyar Jhukta Nahin*. The film wasn't nearly as big a hit as most Sridevi films in the Tamil industry. By now, big bad Bollywood was taking up most of her time. *Himmatwala* had proved to be a massive money spinner and made her a national sensation. More blockbuster Telugu remakes followed and films like *Jaani Dost, Justice Chaudhury, Mawaali, Tohfa, Maqsad* and *Masterji* only added to the aura. 1986 and 1987 were big years, with her moving out of remake territory and headlining 'original' Hindi films (whatever that means) like *Nagina, Sultanat, Bhagwaan Dada* and finally, *Mr India*. By now, she was the biggest female superstar this country had ever seen. The whole nation went weak on the knees; everyone was a Sridevi fan.

It no longer made any sense to work in languages which wouldn't give her nationwide reach. But there were a handful of exceptions. She did come back in the '90s to do a handful Telugu films with K. Raghavendra Rao and Ram Gopal Varma, and a Malayalam film with Bharathan (as mentioned previously).

After the triumphant ride of *Kshana Kshanam* Ram Gopal Varma schemed another Telugu spectacle, this time casting her with Nagarjuna in *Govinda Govinda*. It starts with an incident concerning Lord Vishnu, his consort Lakshmi and Sage Bhrigu, which ends in Lakshmi leaving their abode (Vaikuntha) in a huff. A mad occultist from Bangkok is looking to steal Lord Venkateswara's crown from the temple in Tirumala, which will help him rule over the known universe. Sridevi is an NRI from Bangkok who travels to Tirumala and befriends a conman-turned-taxi-driver, Nagarjuna. There is also a little boy who is actually Lord Venkateswara in disguise. There are too many strands to this story, but Sridevi carries it on her shoulders like nobody's business. *Kshana Kshanam* and *Govinda Govinda* saw RGV at the peak of his creativity, and Sridevi amps it up with oomph and sheer comic timing. RGV and Sridevi were a fantastic team, and it's a pity they didn't make more films together. The film got some decent reviews but ran into a lot of controversies due to the depiction of Lord Venkateswara. Even then, religion and mythology in cinema really riled people up. *Govinda Govinda* had some fantastic, lilting music including 'Amma Brahma Devudu' which RGV inserted as his ode to his goddess. Similar to the fate of *Govinda Govinda*, Sridevi's last outing in Telugu also couldn't set the cash registers ringing.

S.P. Parasuram had a lot going for it. It had Sridevi and Chiranjeevi on the back of the mammoth success of *Jagadeka Veerudu Athiloka Sundari*; the songs were composed by M.M. Keeravani; and it was the 'massy' kind of action potboiler with an honest, angry police officer at the helm (Chiranjeevi). The Telugu film was an official remake of the Tamil *Walter Vetrivel* starring Sathyaraj and Sukanya. This was also remade in Hindi as *Khuddar* featuring Govinda and Karisma Kapoor. Both of those films turned superhits, but *S.P. Parasuram* tanked. Unlike the other versions in which the female leads played stage performers, Sridevi portrayed a rather ravishing thief in the film.

Devaraagam was the last film Sridevi featured in, in a South Indian language. A glorious journey that began way back in 1969 had taken a very different turn. From 1983 onwards, the woman blazed a trail right through Bollywood in a way that has not been matched ever since. In the beginning of the book, I mentioned how this journey began with a love story. It also culminated in a love story, in a manner of speaking.

Boney Kapoor noticed her for the first time in a Tamil movie, back in the 1970s. He was instantly enamoured with her and wanted to cast her in a Hindi film, one of his own productions. He even had a male lead in mind. He was thinking of making a film with Rishi Kapoor. Boney bought the rights to the film, with the intent of showing it to Rishi but that did not happen. He travelled all the way to Madras, with the hopes of meeting her and offering the film. But she was not in town... She was blissfully shooting her next film in Singapore. The film she was shooting for was probably *Priya*. Foreign shoots weren't an everyday event in Tamil cinema, and Singapore featured prominently in this film.

The next time he saw her was in *Solva Sawan*, Bharathiraja's remake of his own Tamil hit *Pathinaru Vayathinile*. The film sank at the box-office but it did leave a trace in Boney Kapoor's mind and heart. He had been unable to take her off his mind. It became an obsession to sign her for a film. The stars aligned and an opportunity presented itself in 1984. Telugu filmmaker Bapu (or Sattiraju Lakshminarayana) was a regular fixture in the films produced by Boney in those days. Bapu had made the first two films for Boney's production house: *Hum Paanch* and *Woh 7 Din*. Bapu had also recently made a film in Telugu with Sridevi and Krishna which was a roaring success, called *Krishnavataram*. Around 1984, Boney signed Bapu to direct a film with Anil Kapoor and Sridevi called *Govinda*. This was also the first time that Boney met Sridevi.

But this was the time a Salim–Javed script called *Mr India* fell into his lap. While *Govinda* was stuck in development hell, Boney put all his energies into mounting *Mr India* which became the first film they worked in together. They interacted on the sets. Somehow the reticent, soft-spoken and rather guarded Sridevi's words reached out to him. Boney and Rajeswari also hit it off from the get-go. It was Rajeswari who used to manage Sridevi's dealings back then.

At the India Today Women's Summit 2013, Boney Kapoor

related an anecdote while Sridevi looked on with a mix of embarrassment and affection wrought on her cherubic face:

> I travelled to Chennai and met her mother. Now, at that point of time she was the highest paid actor among the females. I knew she had signed films for about eight or eight and a half lakh rupees those days. Her mother quoted me ten lakhs. Probably that was her way of negotiating, so I heard her figure and I said... no, I will pay eleven lakhs! She thought I was one bad producer come from Bombay and she probably took a while to react to the reality that somebody out here is offering more than what she asked for. And that's how I got close to her mother.[47]

Throughout his telling of this tale, he was beaming and she tried to stop him from spilling out too many details. During the making of *Mr India*, Boney saw to it that her every comfort was attended to even before she uttered a word. As the shoot progressed, he found himself drawn to her more and more. When she was heading to Switzerland, he followed her there. When her father passed away in 1991, she was shooting for *Lamhe* near Manchester. She rushed back to India, and Boney was there at the airport to receive her. He took care of everything. He was there for the family, and that was something that struck a chord with her. They eventually tied the knot in June 1996. *Judaai* was the last major film she featured in, and then she decided to step out of the studio and into the shadows to make more time for her family. Since her beginnings in 1969 till that day in 1997, for almost three decades she had been continuously

[47]'Boney Kapoor Speaks about Falling in Love with Bollywood Diva, Sridevi', YouTube, https://tinyurl.com/35jaxj48. Accessed on 29 May 2023.

working. There was no break, not even for a single year. She started working at six and took her first break at 34.

⁊

When 'Kingmaker' Kamaraj, and the Kaviarasu Kannadasan led that young girl into the arc-lights, little did they know what they were unleashing. This little girl had a very different kind of school to go to. Playing in the lap of legends, she not only picked up acting but a plethora of languages. Much before she became the darling of the nation by having Bollywood at her feet, she was already almost a veteran in the South.

By the time *Himmatwala* came along, she had been a successful actor for more than a decade. She had already spent 14 years in the movie business. Her co-star Jeetendra had spent 19. Bollywood gave her nationwide fame, but the 1980s were the most creatively impoverished period in the history of Hindi cinema. The heroine had precious little to do. She was either an oversexed arm-candy or a maudlin housewife. All of this she could do in her sleep. All the Tamil, Telugu and Malayalam films that she did growing up had been her training ground.

Tamil films especially gave her the scope to train her acting muscles. At 12 years, she played her first major grown-up role with the unusual story of a woman thirsting for revenge (*Moondru Mudichu*). At 13 she played a 16-year-old who overcomes the most traumatic obstacles and eventually 'comes of age' (*Pathinaru Vayathinile*). The very next year she was part of two films where her boyfriend was a serial killer (*Sigappu Rojakkal*), and where her husband secretly shoots porn (*Gayathri*).

Her first significant role in a Malayalam cinema (a

language she didn't speak) was also the one that got her, her first award for acting when she was barely seven years old. While she was a teenager, she teamed up with Kamal Haasan on a plethora of Malayalam films (*Aadhya Paadam, Aasheervaadam, Sathyavan Savithri* and *Nirakudam*); and with I.V. Sasi—one of the most formidable figures in mainstream Malayalam cinema—she collaborated on 10 films. Almost as soon as she started doing lead roles she established herself as a bankable star, teaming up with the reigning superstars like NTR, Krishna and ANR. She played NTR's granddaughter and in a matter of years, featured in prominent blockbusters as his love interest. She was ANR's heroine and then his son Nagarjuna's heroine. She formed the longest and most successful stint of a leading pair with Krishna.

When the film magazines in Bombay were hailing the 'new find' from the South after *Himmatwala* became a hit, she was already a prominent star. Little did the Hindi filmwallahs know, or care. What they offered were trifles for an actor who could (and had) upstaged some of the most accomplished thespians of the South and, by extension of India. The more 'serious' filmmakers of Hindi cinema never considered her. (Or she never considered them.) I wish they had seen *Moondru Mudichu, Manitharil Ithanai Nirangala* or *Pathinaru Vayathinile.* History would have shaped up differently.

Sridevi passed away on the evening of 24 February 2018. It was a shock most Indians were ill-equipped to handle. The fact that she died in a country so far away and the circumstances surrounding her demise, continue to fuel speculation and conspiracy theories. She was all of 54 when she died. She had done almost 200 films in Tamil, Telugu, Malayalam and Kannada—most of them much before she made a name for herself in Hindi. Those are the movies where she truly pushed the envelope, where the actor in her really flourished. She was an actor, way before the world made her a diva. We do her a disservice by celebrating the latter while ignoring the former. I think the fans (especially her Bollywood fans) will do well to find and watch some of the films she did in South Indian languages, now that so many of them are available on YouTube and on other platforms with subtitles. That would be a more respectful way to remember, and celebrate, this legend.

Part II

The Interviews

An Interview with Baradwaj Rangan: 'The Film Industry was a University for Her'

When I first understood the distinction between a film reviewer and a film critic, I realized there weren't too many of the latter in India. Baradwaj Rangan is a glowing exception to this. I have been following his work for years, so it was a fanboy moment when I got to meet him at his office in Chennai and talk films. This interview was conducted on 30 July 2019.

AR: I find it very interesting that between five to 34 years, Sridevi worked continuously without a break. The first real break came when she got married. But before that, it's so amazing. There's not even a one-year break. In the same year, 1976, she was playing a kid and she was doing *Moondru Mudichu* which is where she played her first adult role.

Baradwaj Rangan: She was 13 or something like that.

AR: Yeah, totally. 13, yes.

Baradwaj Rangan: I don't think she was a very natural actress if that's what you mean. When you name Shabana or Smita, I was a little surprised because that Realistic School of acting was never hers. She was always from the Navarasa School of acting, where everything was a little exaggerated for commercial effect. And I mean this in a nice way because that's just a different style. So, I don't think she was realistic as an actress but she could kind of be convincing about whatever emotion she wanted to play. And I think, you know, she had certain ticks that she did very well. Like she would let her lower lip quiver and, you know, she would put water on herself to suggest sweat in a tense moment or something. Those are some things that she did. But overall, she was a very good commercial film actress and I say this as an opposite to, say, a Smita Patil who was not a very good commercial film actress. She kind of floundered in that zone. You know, she was very uncomfortable with it. Like when you see her in that song from *Shakti* 'Humne Sanam ko Khat Likha'. She's trying but something's not coming through, you know, and in this zone Sridevi knew her way around.

AR: And considering that she had zero training in acting apart from seeing all these big stars on the set, it's very strange how comfortable she was in *Moondru Mudichu* and those early films.

Baradwaj Rangan: You have to keep in mind the directors of that time. K. Balachander, Bharathiraja...all those people were also very skilled. KB, in fact was renowned for making debutantes act. He has introduced so many people who are now thriving in their careers. He introduced Rajinikanth, he introduced the adult Kamal Haasan in his movies—Kamal was a child artist before that. He has introduced so many actors and actresses. So, I'm pretty sure that he knew what to do with her. So, what I'm trying to say is that once she knew how to play those cues, I think she kind of developed her own little repertoire. I remember the actress Shripriya saying that even during shoots when they were together, they would invite her to join them but she'd always say 'yes' and then go off alone to read a book or something like that. So, I think that was what she was. She was very intuitive. Kamal Haasan said that [...] she had an excellent bag of tricks. Which is really a necessity for commercial cinema because you kind of need to know what to do. Kamal is a very intuitive performer and when he's throwing things at you, you need to be able to respond. Its almost like playing tennis, because you don't know where the ball is going to go, you have to be alert. And she was all of that because you find very few heroines who are able to match the intuitive things that Kamal Haasan does and she was definitely one of them.

AR: So, the three of them...would it be right to say that the three of them practically grew up together? Of course there's an age difference, but Rajinikanth, Kamal Haasan and Sridevi seemed to be struggling and growing together in the movies around the same time... Not age-wise but in terms of the roles that they were graduating into.

Baradwaj Rangan: I would say yes, because I think with Kamal she acted in some 20–25 plus films, and around the same with Rajini also. You know, today when people act in movies they say this *jodi* [couple] has already been seen and we need a fresh pair etc., but back then it wasn't like that. Prem Nazir and Sheila did some hundred films, or something like that, in Malayalam cinema. But people didn't care. They were like, people love this pair. Let's just put them on. So yeah, they kind of grew together. Except that I would say Kamal Haasan came in with *Arangetram* which was earlier, say probably '73-ish; Rajini came in with *Apoorva Raagangal* which is I think was in '75, and then *Moondru Mudichu*.

AR: Kamal Haasan's first adult role was in *Apoorva Raagangal...*?

Baradwaj Rangan: No. I think he was clearly an adolescent in *Arangetram*. But he also played a bit of a playboy in *Sollathan Ninaikiren*. I'm talking about all Balachander films. But I would say, he was not the lead in *Moondru Mudichu* it was more like a cameo. So, I would say maybe his first hero role in Tamil cinema was probably *Apoorva Raagangal*. He was the leading man.

AR: These guys so seamlessly did a negative role, then a lead role and then again a negative role.

Baradwaj Rangan: This was because at that point their 'images' were not set. So, I think one of the interesting things in Rajinikanth's career was a movie called *Bhuvana Oru Kelvikkuri*. Rajini plays the good guy and Sivakumar plays the bad guy [this was in contrast to the roles they normally played those days. Sivakumar usually played positive characters while Rajini played negative roles]. In the early part of his career, Rajini was cast in a lot of roles with grey shades, but they were just playing around. It's only after their images got set with a series of superhits that Rajini–Kamal kind of decided they couldn't be doing this much more.

AR: This is roughly around the '80s?

Baradwaj Rangan: '81–'82. Like for Rajini it was *Murattu Kaalai* and for Kamal it was *Sakalakala Vallavan*. And these two movies made them gigantic stars. And Rajini didn't want to experiment much after that, because he figured out that the people were paying to see him in a certain kind of role. Kamal continued to try and experiment all over the place. But yeah, I think that's when stardom happened to them. But before that they were still young, hungry actors who were trying to do a lot of things.

AR: In Hindi cinema, if I talk about the '70s or the '80s, most of the heroines were picked because the role was of a certain kind, projects a certain image or was placed in a certain sort of a genre. But with Sridevi specifically and these bunch of films: *Pathinaru Vayathinile, Gayathri* and even *Moondru Mudichu*. They were not conventional heroine-type roles. Is it about that particular era? Is it about the filmmakers specifically? Or is it about Tamil cinema in general, that women at that period were given slightly edgy kind of roles.

Baradwaj Rangan: So, what you call the 'edgy kind of roles' was because of the stories that were being made at that point. Because nobody said, this will work and that won't work. There was a certain melodrama template that really worked. And so, it was okay for a heroine to play an exploited wife where the husband films her having sex—which is the *Gayathri* story. I mean, today you can't imagine a heroine doing it because she would be worried about her image and things like that but back then people just did it because it was a good role. And that's kind of what the cinema of the time was, you know, till about the '90s I would say. In the '70s, Prameela played a sex worker. Sujatha, Sridevi, all of them played very, very different kind of roles from what the conventional heroine template was and you could say a lot of the filmmakers were interested in making films in which women had interesting parts to play. But once this Rajinikanth kind of stardom happened, you know, the hero became so larger than life that the heroine gradually began to get pushed down the ladder. So, it's only a few filmmakers like K. Balachander who still continued to make women-oriented films.

AR: And these were essentially commercial films, so to speak, mainstream cinema?

Baradwaj Rangan: Yeah, they were mainstream. Tamil cinema has no art film tradition.

AR: That's what I have heard.

Baradwaj Rangan: Like Adoor Gopalakrishnan, Aravindan or Gathak…we never had that. We never had a movement like that. So all of it is various shades of mainstream, from the slightly arty to wholesale masala or whatever but it's never been non-mainstream in Tamil cinema.

AR: Which is interesting, given the plot of these films particularly. Were these commercially successful?

Baradwaj Rangan: To a reasonable extent. It's difficult to know now, but they are still remembered so I would say they all made some kind of impression. But it must also be remembered that the budgets were so low that they didn't require to become huge blockbusters to kind of get back their money. *Pathinaru Vayathinile* was a blockbuster. That was a huge, huge hit. Bharathiraja's first three or four films were huge blockbusters. But I'm less sure about films like *Gayathri* and *Moondru Mudichu* because Balachander had a core niche audience and he also kept his budgets so low that I don't think he needed the blockbuster kind of successes.

AR: Okay. So in terms of filmmakers would I be right if I say that the key filmmakers, as far as Sridevi's Tamil filmography was concerned, in Tamil cinema were K. Balachander, Bharathiraja, Balu Mahendra and Mahendran.

Baradwaj Rangan: Yeah. But I wouldn't say key filmmakers, because she hasn't acted in too many films by them. She has acted in two films with Bharathiraja: *Sigappu Rojakkal* and *Pathinaru Vayathinile*. With Mahendran in one film, *Johnny*. With Balu Mahendra just one film, *Moondram Pirai;* and with

KB, *Moondru Mudichu* and *Varumayin Niram Sivappu*. So I don't know...I won't say key filmmakers. I will just say they were important. You know, I think she worked with a gamut of people. She worked with all these directors who were on this side of mainstream and she worked with directors on the other side of mainstream as well, like S.P. Muthuraman. So, she could do everything that they wanted. She was working like a maniac and I think she just worked with everybody that got her a good role.

AR: Because I have only seen a handful of her films and given that so little is available with subtitles, which are the important or significant films that I should cover? I have a very small list. I have *Moondru Mudichu, Pathinaru Vayathinile, Gayathri, Kavikkuyil, Meendum Kokila*. And of course, *Moondram Pirai*.

Baradwaj Rangan: I would say *Moondru Mudichu, Gayathri, Pathinaru Vayathinile, Manidharil Ithanai Nirangala* because that's a very interesting story with Sri and Kamal, but they're not like a pair. Because Kamal is her best friend's husband. So, then I would say cover *Dharma Yuddham*. She plays a reporter and Rajinikanth is also there. And I would say cover *Pagalil Oru Iravu* because there is a very interesting role that she plays where she's traumatized by sexual experiences. And there is a very graphic song shot on her. Not exactly graphic, but she's wearing a very short skirt. The camera kind of goes all over the place and it's pretty vulgar to see it these days. So, I mean, like, she's very young and here is the older hero who's literally grazing on her. *Johnny*...you want to see *Johnny* because that's a really well-known performance with Rajini. *Meendum Kokila* and *Vazhve Mayam* maybe, because it was one of the biggest blockbusters...and *Moondram Pirai*.

AR: After that there was *Himmatwala* and then there was practically nothing.

Baradwaj Rangan: Suhasini Maniratnam told me once that Mahendran did something very interesting in *Johnny*. Johnny [Rajinikanth] is actually a criminal and he doesn't want to marry Archana [Sridevi] because she's an innocent singer. She falls for him and he doesn't want to marry her. She thinks that he is not marrying her because she's an artist and, you know, artists are supposed to have loose morals and things like that. And then she starts getting emotional. And he says, 'No, no, it's not like that.' Then finally, they get married and in that scene Mahendran wanted them to sort of cut each other off and not speak the full lines, you know. Like, I'm telling you one thing and instead of waiting for me to finish my line you cut me off...that kind of thing, and Suhasini said Sridevi got it like that *[snaps fingers]*! But Rajini struggled a bit with that because he was used to hearing the whole line and then responding with his line because that's the traditional model of acting. So, she was very good with picking up things like that.

AR: I don't know how to articulate this, but do you really believe she was just walking into these sets and doing these roles one after the another robotically? How and from where did this sophistication come? You know, she was just playing child roles and she was just from this small town.

Baradwaj Rangan: I think these things she picked up along the way. I don't think there was any great formative influence that you can point to. It's not like there's one phase where she's terrible and then suddenly this director came into her life and she transformed overnight. She is a very mysterious kind of actor because she didn't speak much. We don't know much about her or her process. We don't know much about the directors or what they said or didn't say. And she didn't exist at a time where there were many interviews around craft and things like that.

AR: Interesting. With Madhubala and Meenakumari who were both child actors, there was a break when they were graduating to adult roles.

Baradwaj Rangan: That's what I'm saying. You can't say time helped her and you can't say somebody specific helped her. The film industry became a university for her. And each person that she came into contact with, she picked something from them and just went on to the next role and then the next role...

AR: Would it be right to say that she was not very self aware while learning these things? Maybe she was imbibing things very organically?

Baradwaj Rangan: Even later I don't think she was very self aware because I get the feeling that she was not a very conscious-method kind of actress.

AR: During the promotion of *Mom* and *English Vinglish*, various interviewers were asking the kind of questions that people normally ask nowadays, which is craft related. The kind of questions that weren't asked earlier. She did not seem very comfortable answering those. I mean, not that anyone caught her on the wrong foot but she probably seemed like someone who didn't give a thought to these things.

Baradwaj Rangan: Or maybe she didn't know how to explain it. You know, it's like some writers can talk about their work but some writers cannot. I think it might be something like that.

An Interview with
G. Dhananjayan:
'She was an Enigma'

G. Dhananjayan is a revered name in film academia and he is an authority in Indian cinema, especially Tamil. He is a writer and film critic with two National Awards in his kitty; has served as producer with Moser Baer and Disney–UTV; and has acted in and produced several films. He has also been heading the South Indian film business wing of Disney UTV Motion Pictures. This interview was taken on 1 August 2019.

AR: I have been researching on her parents. I know about her mother's acting career, and the films she acted in. But I don't seem to find a lot of information on her father. Can you talk about her parents a little, and her early days?

G. Dhananjayan: Both her father and mother were actively into politics. They were in the Congress. At that time in Congress party, everyone used to bring their kids to the functions—election meetings and stuff. She was in a meeting where Kamaraj and Kannadasan were there. It's Kannadasan who gave her the name Sridevi. Her name was not Sridevi. He is the one who gave her that name. Kannadasan was the great poet and lyricist, he got a national award and he was one of the biggest poets of Tamil film industry. You know he called her Sridevi and he was the one who recommended to Thevar, the producer saying that there is a kid, you know... who can play Lord Muruga. He said, 'Why don't you cast her?' That's when a five-year-old kid was cast as Muruga and she acted in this particular film, *Thunaivan.* You know, her father didn't like that she was made to join films. In fact, that is when the father and the mother separated—when she was brought to cinema. So, after that you will rarely see any photos of her with her father. Rarely any photo would have appeared of Sridevi with both her mother and father. It was the mother who took Sridevi away and started grooming her for cinema. He, on the other hand, was a reputed politician. He didn't want it. See, here cinema is still seen as a last resort for those who have no other thing to do. So, what really happened here is that, her father felt that he was a reputed politician and unnecessarily his girl was getting exposed to cinema. He didn't want to get her into that. But the mother was very attached to cinema. She liked cinema and she wanted her daughter to come into cinema and Kannadasan was the main influence because he was close to the family. He said she's cute, get her into acting. And that was the time Kamal Haasan was also making a splash around 1965.

AR: He must be very...I mean, he must be a child actor at the time!

G. Dhananjayan: Yes, you know those days three kids were making splashes everywhere. One was Daisy Irani, one was Kamal Haasan and then there was this kid. And then you know, everybody noticed that these are the future stars. Kamal Haasan came in '65, Sridevi came in '69 and Daisy came in '65. Kannadasan felt that she has the required charisma so why shouldn't she be in the movies? That's why she came in, but the father didn't like it. They moved to Chennai. [...] After that they never went back to their roots. Basically, they were very close knit till she came into the movies. You know, she is the only person who grew up on the sets. No other actor grew up like that.

AR: It's really amazing if you think of it, because whenever I think of a successful child artist who grew up as a successful actress, I kind of think of Madhubala and Meena Kumari... but even they had a break. There wasn't a single year in her growing up years when Sridevi wasn't working. So in 1976, in the same year, she was doing an adult role in *Moondru Mudichu* and she was a child artiste in so many other films! I find that so amazing. So fascinating.

G. Dhananjayan: You know, this happened only because she started loving cinema. She never went to school. See, when she started she was a toddler. Now what happened is, from then on she was continuously acting in films. 1969 onwards she was acting in various languages and everywhere she was so cute! She never had any inhibition because she was an actor. If you see the stills from '71 and all you will be amazed by the girl being such a dedicated kid, playing Muruga. Then, in '75, [...] she was a heroine. All this while, she was continuously acting as a child artiste. Then at the age of 13, she got cast by K. Balachander [...]in *Moondru Mudichu*, where she plays a grown-up. [...] I don't know, this was magic. If you see, she never looked old because she was like a child. Her body changed but her face never changed. Her face was just like a child. So beautiful, so innocent, so childlike. And she never studied, but she learned everything on her own. You know whether it is English, whether it is any language, [...] even Hindi. She never went to school. Kamal

Haasan at that time was also a child artist. He took a break for five years and then came back. He was always watching her. They were child artists, they were working together. Now from *Moondru Mudichu* to every other film, they were acting together. When she was 14, he was 17–18.[48] So, they had like a four-year gap. Again, in the same film, Rajinikanth was also there. Then she came in *Pathinaru Vayathinile* ('At the age of 16' is what the title means). When that film came, she was not even 16! She was 15 years old. And here she was acting in a film called *Pathinaru Vayathinile* but her look is not of 15 years. Yeah, that's the transformation of the girl. Because she was only into cinema. She was always thinking about cinema…eating, thinking, everything was about cinema. Her body changed to suit that particular character. You have to see from the point of view of this girl, she never had any problems taking risks. She would take risks in career. She acted in very unconventional, bold films. As per the demand of the character, she transformed; she switched into that particular role. And similarly, when she was acting in *Moondru Mudichu*, she was transforming into a woman and a mother at the age of 13–14. Acted like a mother to Rajinikanth and acted as the wife of a 65-year-old. She had no worry at all. She had the guts to do any bloody role. She felt very clearly: 'I am born to act'.

AR: So, this is my second question actually. *Moondru Mudichu, Gayathri, Pathinaru Vayathinile,* all of these were in many ways pathbreaking. *Gayathri* was a role that even today if one were to make it in Hindi with, you know, Kangana Ranaut or someone like that even by 2019 standards, it will be a very bold and edgy role, right?

---

[48]Kamal Haasan and Sridevi had an age gap of nine years.

G. Dhananjayan: Absolutely.

AR: How did she, a person who was not well read, by my understanding, do it? She obviously didn't see a lot of world cinema. She didn't go to any film institute. She didn't get exposed to a whole lot of great foreign actors, like Marlon Brando or whatever, right? She didn't know method acting, of course. How did a person like that get into that level of sophistication to take on a role like *Moondru Mudichu* where she's playing mother to a person who is already in his own way, almost becoming a star right then? Rajinikanth was well on his way to become a star. He wasn't a star yet, but he was on his way. To play a role like that, to play a role like *Gayathri*, how could she even understand what the director was saying? That kind of sophistication at that young age? How did that transition happen?

G. Dhananjayan: I think a lot of directors who worked with her told me that she was a 'switch on/switch off' actor. When the camera was on, they said that a *bhoot* [ghost] gets inside her and that bhoot is acting. That bhoot [...] transforms her completely into somebody else. The moment the cameras are off, she has no idea what happened.

AR: She is just like a normal person.

G. Dhananjayan: She didn't have any idea is what a lot of directors told me. They are not able to explain how this transformation happens to her. When you spoke to her, she appeared very ordinary; very normal. She was not well aware...it's exactly like what you're saying. She hadn't read. She had no idea. Cinema never went out of her. Because, from the age of seven years you're on the set. You're innocent. You never went out. You never saw the world and you had a comfortable life. She was getting a lot of money.

She was fed with a lot of food and juice and everything. She was protected by mother [sic]. She was always with her mother. She slept on the mother's lap. She was sleeping on her mother's lap till the age of 40. Till she got married to Boney Kapoor, she was only sleeping on mother's lap. Can you believe it? She never went outside.

AR: She never partied?

G. Dhananjayan: She never partied. She never went out with any hero. She always cuddled with the mother and slept in the bed. Now we all know very clearly in the Tamil film industry that she would always hold her mother's hand when she arrived. She never came alone. She would never stand alone. And she would never give any interviews.

AR: I've heard her mother took most of her decisions.

G. Dhananjayan: [...] The only reason her mother took the decision is because she was a 'switch on/switch off' actor. Any role given to her, she would do. See what really happens is, you know that from the age of seven you've been taught by legend directors. She was taught by the likes of A.P. Nagarajan and a lot of other directors. She acted with Sivaji Ganesan. Did you know, she acted as his daughter, then as his sister...and then as his romantic lead in a number of films?

AR: She played daughter as well as heroine to a number of actors...Krishna, Sivaji Ganesan, Akkineni Nageswaro Rao.

G. Dhananjayan: She is unbelievable. I'll tell you what... you cannot really compare her with anybody. I just don't admire her, I say that she is God's gift to cinema. Nobody can actually define it any other way. Like how God instructs some special talents sometimes: 'Go, I'm blessing you; go do this and come back.' Here, you know, God has given us so many people. Ramanujan is one such example. He came, gave us mathematics and went away pretty soon. Yes, like this in Tamil Nadu and [sic] we have got Pattukkottai Kalyanasundaram. The man lives through his lyrics even today. He passed away 60 years ago. Bharathiyar (celebrated Tamil poet Subramania Bharathi) passed away at the age of 39. And today, he's like a legendary poet. And that's how she is too. Bharathiyar was a poet, nobody knows how he did it and what his process was. And just like that, Sridevi has become a cult actress. That's all I know, they all are blessed by God. Can you define her acting? No! The only thing you can say is that she was well trained by legendary directors because she acted in a lot of such films. But she never got an opportunity to reflect upon it herself.

AR: So, it's very organic. It came naturally to her.

G. Dhananjayan: Absolutely.

AR: So nowadays, there is this trend, almost every other journalist...everybody is constantly talking about craft and all of that which didn't happen in those days. Recently, I remember after *English Vinglish* [...] she had to do a lot of interviews and it was apparent that she was being forced because she was not a very extroverted kind of a person. So, she was asked all of these modern-day questions about craft and how do you do it? What was your approach, and she was always kind of...she was not really caught on the wrong foot, but she genuinely didn't have a strong answer for that. Even on the Vir Sanghvi interview he was asking about it, and she said 'No, I just did it.' I mean, to somebody who studies so many actors, it's so strange...but now that you compare with a poet it makes sense. She was probably very, very organic. So when you ask her, how could she have answered? She didn't have an answer for it, because even she can't explain it. It just happened.

G. Dhananjayan: See another probable example is like, say, of Kannadasan. You go and tell him a situation. Immediately he'll just think about it and give you a poem. And most of the people even today are not able to fathom how he got that poem. His lyrics came just like that. A lot of people 'engineer' lyrics. They look at the tune, they look at a word, 'Oh, no, this will not sit with the tune…' and then they write another word. I saw once the way Kannadasan did it. I was amazed. He'd hear a tune and go '*Ah, yeiduko* (Ok, write)'. And it fit in perfectly to the situation! Sridevi is like that. She's a born genius. She did it organically. That's the reason why a lot of it just happened. If you go and ask her to intellectualize it…maybe Kamal Haasan would intellectualize it, if you go and ask him. He's a self-aware actor, he's a methodical actor. But Sridevi was born genius. I'm not saying this negatively, of course. I'm saying it positively. Kamal Haasan developed it, because he watched a lot of world cinema. He learned from actors like Marlon Brando and others. He developed a style for himself, he trained himself. Sridevi didn't bother at all. She was living on the sets. She just developed on her own. And a lot of people kept telling her do this, do that […] and she kept on improving. So somewhere the credit, you know, will go to the legendary directors and actors. She acted with a lot of legendary actors, so she knew how they performed. And she would immediately pick it up. The only difference is a lot of people will act outside also, this girl would not act on the outside. When the switch went on, she would act…switch off, and she doesn't know what to do. That's the reason when she is asked, she doesn't know how to explain the whole process. Now how did she go about taking risks? It was actually her mother who took the risks. The mother felt that the career of a heroine is usually very short. Now, she looked cute and she got very good offers and her mother felt it's important that she acts in as many films as possible. And she knew Telugu very well...because at home they spoke Telugu, it was her mother tongue. So she automatically got into Telugu cinema. She was doing a lot of them. She didn't know Malayalam. She did those films mainly because she got opportunities there. She also did a few Kannada films. Hindi came in much later. If in all the four language industries she became a queen, it was because the mother felt that these are good opportunities and she let her act. So she was continuously acting every day. One day acting in a Telugu film set, one day at a Tamil film set and then a Malayalam film set...it just went on like that. Her mother was deciding everything and she had no role to play. She just did as she was told. She said, 'Okay, since you've chosen I will do it. I don't care what the role is.' And then she went and did what the director told her to do. She could pick up the character instantly and she would do it. And you'll also see that there was an enormous consistency in her roles. Like if she picks up a role, she will know how to consistently deliver the goods. That was her in-born quality. It's not that because she was working in Telugu cinema and then in Tamil cinema, there was any inconsistency. No. She was very clear about her role. The best thing about her, if you ask me, was that she was completely dedicated to cinema. She never had any outside life. She was in the set all 24 hours. She was acting around the clock and right from 1969!

AR: There's no break. The first break came when she got

married. Before that there was not even one year.

G. Dhananjayan: She was continuously acting, almost around 300 films. You know, she was crazy about acting and it was never just about the money. At one stage, you know, she made enough money that she was the reigning queen. But then, you know, for her cinema was everything. She didn't know anything else. She was only pursuing cinema, cinema, cinema. So that's what Sridevi was. She was an enigma.

AR: Absolutely. So I was watching this short video clip from *Thunaivan.* She's not there throughout the film. She appears in the climax, for a very small portion. So, there's this scene with these two people who are Murugan's devotees and it is a very heightened emotion...so they faint and she's kind of ringing the bell with the chain. This small kid who is, you know, swinging the chains like this. I'm sure she did not have the strength to swing the bell. It was just shown like that... but even at that age, she seemed to have a natural flair for being on camera. Any other kid of that age won't even know where to look. But she knew and she was a natural. She went around talking to people and she had the confidence that one would think a deity to have [...] One would expect a certain confidence, for a character like that. And she had that flamboyance and personality at the age of four! So amazing.

G. Dhananjayan: Yeah, she was like that. That's why I said she was God's child. Nobody can define her. It's very difficult to define her as a character. And in fact she remained an enigma in Tamil cinema, because she was not really close to anybody. She never had any interaction with anybody. She never had any friends. She never had friends at all.

AR: Speaking of friends, would it be right to say that Kamal Haasan, Rajinikanth and Sridevi—despite the difference in their ages—kind of grew up together in cinema, struggling together? Would it be right to say that?

G. Dhananjayan: She grew up with Kamal. But Rajini came in much later. She grew up with Kamal because they were on the sets all the time together and that's how they were growing up.

An Interview with Chitra Lakshmanan: 'They Even Criticized the Saris She Wore'

Chitra Lakshmanan wears many hats. As a director, producer, actor and journalist, he has spent many years as an industry insider in the Tamil film industry. This makes him uniquely placed as a storehouse of information and anecdotes. He hosts a celebrity chat show called *Chai with Chitra* and a cinema podcast on Spotify. The following interview was taken on 31 July 2019.

AR: Would it be fair to say that the three of them—Kamal Haasan, Sridevi and Rajinikanth—were almost growing together, not in terms of age but in terms of their acting? Were three of them friends?

Chitra Lakshmanan: Yes yes, sure. But Kamal and Sridevi vibed much better as actors. Her first film *Moondru Mudichu* plays a very important part in her career, and it was important for Rajinikanth also. Were you able to see it? It's a wonderful film.

AR: Yes, that's a wonderful film. That's fortunately one of the handful of films from that period which is available with subtitles. I thoroughly enjoyed it. It's a very different concept. As a matter of fact, the story idea and the concept of *Gayathri*, is also very unconventional. So, I'd like to know: was it also unconventional in terms of Tamil cinema or was everybody in that era experimenting and doing films like that?

Chitra Lakshmanan: No, what you say is correct. It was an unconventional movie. It was a novel written by Sujatha, a popular writer who has been associated with Shankar [director] in all his films till Sujatha died. In films like *Enthiran, Sivaji: The Boss* etc., he had a very big role to play. He wrote the dialogues.

AR: Sujatha was also the writer who wrote a series of novels about a couple of lawyers. I think the film was *Priya*.

Chitra Lakshmanan: Yes, Ganesh–Vasanth. *Priya* was made in Tamil and in Kannada. In the Kannada version Ambareesh did the main role. And Rajini played the second fiddle there. Here [in Tamil] Rajini was prominent, Ambareesh did the secondary role. *Gayathri* had a lot of controversial reviews also. Even Sujatha said that when it was published there was a lot of criticism. He wasn't sure how the film would be made.

AR: Was it a book by Sujatha?

Chitra Lakshmanan: Yes, Sujatha wrote the book. It was actually serialized in a magazine and then it came as out a book as well. When it was serialized, Panchu Arunchalam [renowned writer, lyricist and producer] had the opportunity of reading that series and then he wanted to make it into a film. It was a very different kind of a film.

AR: Even today if somebody had to make it, it would be a very, very bold film.

Chitra Lakshmanan: Rajinikanth at that time was doing only those kinds of roles. He played the main villain in *Gayathri* and that became the turning point for him. Panchu Arunachalam wanted to show the writer Sujatha, how he had visualized his novel on the screen. He took Sujatha along with him and went to the theatre to give the writer a shock. But eventually, it was Panchu Arunachalam himself who learnt a lesson from the theatre. The hero of the film is Jaishankar and Rajinikanth is the villain. But when the hero beats Rajinikanth, people are against Jaishankar...against the hero...and when Rajinikanth beats the hero—when the villain beats the hero—they start clapping and there's a lot of roaring applause. And that's when he understood that Rajinikanth is not just a villain anymore. If there were more films with him as villain, people won't like it. So Rajinikanth had to be cast as a hero thereafter. That is a decision he took in the theatre that day.

AR: So Rajini was a trained actor, right? And he was well in his 20s when this was happening. So, his choice of unconventional roles can still be understood but what I find amazing and sightly puzzling about Sridevi is that she didn't have a formal education in acting. I don't think she was a very avid reader either. Where did this thought process come from? Because somebody like that would just pick up normal commercial song-and-dance kind of movies. Is this just a coincidence?

Chitra Lakshmanan: But there is a big difference between today's cinema and the cinema of the 1980s. See, she was not deciding the films herself. It was her mother. She would only go according to the directions of her mother.

Whatever she [her mother] was saying, she would follow. They even criticized the saris she wore. She would just ask her mother, 'Should I wear green or red?' Whatever her mother said, she would obey. And even her mother didn't have a choice in listening to stories like that. Good [production] company, good producer, big banner, good writer, good director…that's how people were signing films in that period. It's only now that everyone takes three months to listen to a story and then it turns out to be the ultimate flop!

AR: I wasn't familiar with her work in Tamil cinema and Telugu or Malayalam. But when I started reading about them and watching some of her films, I was really shocked because when you look at her Hindi work it's mostly as a commercial dancing heroine in which she was really good, but in her Tamil films…

Chitra Lakshmanan: In Tamil cinema you will see Sridevi as Smita Patil in some films. And likewise, you'll see her as Mumtaz in some films. She didn't have that variation in Hindi.

AR: That's exactly what I told Mr Baradwaj Rangan […]. I said when I look at her, I see an actress of a Mumtaz–Smita Patil level. When you look at her work in Tamil cinema… and maybe a bit of her in Malayalam cinema…she is of a very different stature.

Chitra Lakshmanan: Yes, she was offered such roles. Here people like K. Balachander, R.C. Sakthi were there. Lot of people who moulded her in a lot of different ways. There in Hindi, she was actually used for commercial films and especially her dancing side was explored more.

AR: How was her relation with Kamal Haasan? He did around 30 films with her. Would her films with Kamal be more than that with Rajinikanth?

Chitra Lakshmanan: Yes, both of them were brought up together in films. Rajini's count [of films with Sridevi] is much lesser as compared to Kamal. Rajinkanth was a small-time actor at that time. *Moondru Mudichu* must be his seventh or eighth film, but Sridevi had opportunities like [...] *Pathinaru Vayathinile* with Kamal Haasan in her early days. So she has grown much faster. In *Pathinaru Vayathinile*, Rajinikanth was only playing second fiddle to Kamal because he was the bad guy, so Rajini came a little later but Kamal was already a star at that time. Rajinikanth first met Kamal Haasan in Kalakendra office. He was just picked up to act in a particular scene. It was his first day and Kamal Haasan walks in. Rajini greets him saying, 'I have seen you in *Sollathan Ninaikiren*. It was some extraordinary acting.' Right after *Arangetram*, Kamal did *Sollathan Ninaikiren* with Balachander. It had a powerful role for Kamal. He played a slightly villainous role but that was the main role in the film. So, he was already a star.

AR: So, who were the important directors in Sridevi's Tamil filmography? Bharathiraja did just two films with her...and Balu Mahendra did just one film with her. *Moondram Pirai* and he later remade it in Hindi as *Sadma*.

Chitra Lakshmanan: P.N. Menon made a very good Malayalam film with her. R.C. Sakthi, who gave the first break to Kamal Haasan, did a film with Sridevi called *Manitharil Ithanai Nirangala.*

AR: Even in this film Kamal Haasan is not a traditional hero and Sridevi is not romantically paired opposite him. It was altogether a different concept. Apart from these were there any filmmakers that she repeatedly worked with? Like in Telugu there were K. Raghavendra Rao, K. Bapayya.

Chitra Lakshmanan: S.P. Muthuraman she has worked with. *Kanimuthu Paappa* and *Deiva Kuzhandhaigal.* She played as a child actor in these. Then in *Kavari Maan* she played Sivaji Ganesan's grown-up daughter too. I think she played Sivaji's daughter in many films. She has also played a heroine in a Sivaji film called *Sandhippu* much later, which was a remake of Amitabh Bachchan's *Naseeb.*

AR: What are 5–6 defining films of her in Tamil that I should definitely cover?

Chitra Lakshmanan: *Moondru Mudichu, Pathinaru Vayathinile, Gayathri.* She did one film with A.C. Tirulokchandar, *Vanakkatukuriya Kathaliye.* That was a very different concept. Not a regular style of film. She also did *Babu* with Tirulokchandar as a child star. *Meendam Kokila* was a commercial hit. Sridevi played the role of a Brahmin housewife.

An Interview with Mohan Raman: 'She was the Ideal Director's Material'

Mohan V. Ram, also known as Mohan Raman, wears many hats. He is a film historian, an actor of TV and film, a writer, entrepreneur and management trainer. He has been a part of Tamil entertainment industry for over three decades. He has also been a member of the National Film Awards jury. In addition to Tamil cinema and TV, he has featured in some Hindi films like *Chennai Express* and *Ajab Prem ki Gazab Kahani*. His recent notable outing was in Mani Ratnam's *Ponniyin Selvan* Part I and II. What follows is a boundless, freewheeling conversation with him on Sridevi and her times. This interview was taken on 4 August 2019.

Mohan Raman: As I explained to you, I entered the film industry in 1991. And by that time, she [Sridevi] had stopped doing Tamil cinema. I have not had any interaction with her per se. Mine are more of observations. As a film historian and as a student of film, I have always believed she was an actor when she was in the South and she became a star or a diva when she went to Bollywood. If we analyse the body of her work, we will find that the meaty roles with the weightage of character all came in the early part of her career. The second part is where she became nationally famous. She was the diva, the icon. All that happened but she was not asked to act. She didn't need to act. She just had to be there.

Rarely do you have this combination of both. If you see film heroines, we've had tremendous beauties and we've had tremendous actors. The actors remained actors. There were beautiful actors. Meena Kumari by no means was not beautiful but she was not renowned for her beauty. She was known for acting. Down south we had Savithri and many others. They were all known for their acting talent...that histrionic ability and less for that glamour quotient. Vidya Balan is also one of them. And Sridevi had tremendously long innings in both spheres. As an actor and as a diva or a superstar.

I still feel the star was artificial. Somehow her eyes lacked expression when she was a star. Maybe it did, in occasional scenes here or there in some movies. But in the movies I'm referring to [her films in the South], she was exuding and throwing it out in almost everything. Can you imagine? She was a child actor. So, there was never a question of being afraid of the camera. [She was] utterly comfortable with the camera and utterly comfortable playing someone else.

AR: So, this is something that I find really strange. Not strange in a bad way, but fascinating. *Thunaivan* was her first film where she played Lord Muruga and there's this one scene where this devout couple is lying on the floor of the temple. Lord Muruga appears as a child, as a cherubic child, and she comes in and rings the bell. Obviously, she's too small but the way she does it, the physical act of it, you want to believe that this kid is really shaking this bell...and her face—nothing will tell you that this kid is not experienced or hasn't been with any stars.

Mohan Raman: That's what I said, it came naturally.

AR: And then the preparation, *Moondru Mudichu* and all of that, how did she even understand the complexity of the character that K. Balachander conceived?

Mohan Raman: And imagine, somebody launching themselves as a heroine willing to play the wife of a middle-aged man. See, she never launched herself as a star. She saw the script, she had implicit faith in a director like Mr Balachander, which most of us had. All of us come from his school. We never asked him what this story was or what the next scene was... we just went and did what he asked us to do or actually to be very honest, what he taught us to do. He always preferred to show you what he wanted. He is not somebody who let you really do the role the way you wanted to do it. He did that after you became seasoned. After that he was like, 'This is a scene, you know the dialogues and I know the dialogues... Now show me what you want to do.'

That 'show me what you want to do' came after maybe working with him for 100 episodes in television in my case. So, I'm sure Sridevi must have had the same treatment from him because he was far more of a firebrand in those days. I think she just trusted the director, trusted the script, trusted the potential of the role and went ahead with it. I can't think of any heroine who will accept being Mrs Calcutta Vishwanathan in that film. Yes, there was Kamal Haasan there as well. But that lasted for a brief period in the film.

AR: She plays Rajinikanth's mother. She was a teenager and he was in his late 20s. So, that is also something. Now look at somebody like a Kamal Haasan. By that time, he

was almost a seasoned actor in the sense that he had done
child roles. And he had grown up within the industry; he
had choreographed and assisted Balachander, if I am not
mistaken, in many films. And while doing that, there was
a schooling that was happening. He has spoken about how
he saw Dilip Kumar's films, he saw Marlon Brando and
all of that. So, this is a kind of schooling. I would assume
that while he would pick scripts, there was a certain sort
of strategic approach to it. Similarly, one could see that
with Aamir Khan as well…choosing his scripts carefully. But
Sridevi had neither been schooled formally and nor did she
assist anybody. There was no school of acting she went to.
Are you basically saying that she chose *Moondru Mudichu*
script with that kind of an awareness, knowing that it was
good for her as a launchpad and was she conscious about
this choice?

Mohan Raman: I'm sure she was […] not from the potential
of the role, but from the potential of the director launching
her.

Balachander was by then an icon. So to be launched by
him was something that people dreamt of and to be launched
in a film with Rajinikanth and Kamal Haasan… Of course,
Rajini wasn't that well known back then, but Kamal was. She
probably had the greatest faith in the director and the team,
knowing that this will be a terrific kick-off for her. More
than that, you don't need to be schooled or watch Brando.
You need to have that instinct. See, what is the difference
between the batting of let's say, Virendra Sehwag and Rahul
Dravid? Rahul Dravid is a percentage player—he is a student
of the game. He knows the rules, plays by the book. Keep
your left foot here. Put your head down, shoulder up, bat
coming straight, etc. So, he is schooled in the technique.

Sehwag, Srikanth or any one of them [...] were just sheer instinct and they went and blasted as many runs as the rest of them. So, there are two kinds of people: one who absorbs what is around them to such an extent that they are masters of the subject in a way, like Kamal Haasan or Aamir Khan. And they were able to shape their career.

Sridevi, on the other hand, I think had a tremendous instinct. The way she rang the bell, as you put it, in *Thunaivan*. She just knew what was needed and what she had to do. Her roles in those days...*Pathinaru Vayathinile, Gayathri...*

AR: Even today, in 2019, if somebody were to make it in Hindi, *Gayathri* would be considered a bold subject.

Mohan Raman: Yes! Even *Moondru Mudichu* was a bold subject. It takes a lot of guts, and you will agree that the actresses in Hindi—not the beauty queens—the Smita Patils and Shabanas, they would have accepted something like this. Somehow I think Sridevi instinctively knew that she had to carve a niche for herself as a performer, a performer with exquisite beauty who could carry off glamorous roles if she wanted and she has done that too. You know, I remember talking to Mr Balu Mahendra who was telling me how she was struggling in the initial days of *Moondram Pirai*. There was some part of the body language which she couldn't figure out. They all sat and worked it out. And he said that, if you notice, the time taken for us to blink our eyes differs from that of a child. For a child, it is a slow blink whereas for an adult it's instantaneous. When they wanted that innocence in her, he couldn't get it because she was doing this *[blinks rapidly]*, till they discovered it and then he said, take your time and blink. That is when her eyes...the magic of her eyes is also revealed. So, there was this plethora of great directors who taught her the craft. Balachander,

Bharathiraja, Balu Mahendra...I mean, she worked with every top director.

AR: Also as a child, she was being exposed to the giants of South Indian cinema. I mean, she worked as the daughter and the heroine of Sivaji Ganesan. And then there was Akkineni Nageswara Rao, Krishna, Gemini Ganesan, even MGR. Every day of her life as a child, rather than going to school she was going to the set.

Mohan Raman: She was being groomed. She was watching them. And I think it stood her in good stead because when she decided that it is time to make the transition, she didn't go to Hindi cinema and challenge them as actors. She did everything she needed to do to become a Hindi film heroine. She did it because that desire to reach the top and stay there was probably so well entrenched in her, having worked with the top stars in the South. MGR, Sivaji and Akkineni Nageswara Rao, Krishna and Kamal...there are so many films where, you know, she had literally become a threat to Kamal... Take *Moondram Pirai* for example. Kamal's performance was great but Sridevi matched him, ball to ball, frame to frame. It was a true partnership.

AR: That very rarely happens in India. It's usually either the heroine that overshadows or the hero that overshadows her.

Mohan Raman: This was ball to ball. And I think she was also lucky that her co-stars all recognized the great talent in her and didn't try to suppress it by cutting off scenes, either during shoot or in post production. And it's not like she didn't do the masala films here. She was equally at ease with that, prancing around the trees and all that.

AR: Which she was predominantly doing in Telugu...?

Mohan Raman: Even in Tamil, if you see, after a while she started doing the regular heroine roles. Maybe because it was Sridevi, they gave her a little more to do than any other heroine would have got. She was the ideal director's material. She allowed herself to be moulded, shaped into the character and lived the character. That's why I said she was an actor when she was in the South. And she became a star when she joined Hindi films.

AR: Completely. In *Moondru Mudichu* and or other early films she had a certain approach which was the K. Balachander school. But when she comes to the Mahendran school in *Johnny*...I probably can't explain. She was more mature—if I can say that. In the romantic scenes, it was not your carried-away mushy romance. It was kind of what you see between Naseer and Shabana in *Sparsh* and films like that. It is a very mature kind of romance, and both Rajini and her were toe-to-toe as with Kamal in *Moondram Pirai*. It is a beautiful performance.

Mohan Raman: Amazing. And while it was one of Mahendran's good films, I'm not going to call it his best. But Mahendran, Balu Mahendra, their school of filmmaking was later adopted by Mani Ratnam. She would have been absolutely at ease with somebody like him because she was director's material. She was not fixated, saying that this is my pattern of acting and I will follow only that. No. 'I am an actor, I will do what you want me to do...what you think this character will do...provided I'm convinced that this is what the character will do.' Because if you deliver an unconvincing performance that will also be seen on-screen, and I don't think she ever allowed herself to do a role which she was not convinced about. So even if it was a mushy romance or masala film, she did it because she was convinced that she is delivering something that no one else can. There is this famous reference to her eyes by this comedian called Thengai Srinivasan. He was the villain in *Dharma Yuddham*... he was into organ smuggling or something like that and he kept saying 'black roses'. He called her eyes 'black roses'. See, I remember that famous statement by K. Balachander about Srividya not Sridevi. He said that I don't need a set, I don't need a backdrop. As long as Srividya's eyes are there, I can work with them.

I think the same could be said of Sridevi. It is equally applicable to her as it is to Srividya. Her early roles, early grooming or, as you said very correctly, exposure to the top people of the South Indian film industry at a very young age...she must have also observed how someone like a Sivaji Ganesan or an MGR chose films. The choice was made with different parameters and I think she merged both. And so when she went there, to the North—to the Hindi film industry she probably made more of the MGR kind of choices, where she said, 'This is the way I can reach the masses.' And when it came to Sivaji, it was more about the role and the acting. So, she was groomed in both commercial cinema and the cinema which is meant for the actors. She kind of had the best of both worlds at a young age and later she was able to draw on that experience and do the needful. Now the question is, could she have stayed on here? I think she would have had much better roles.

AR: Yeah! It is a pity that Mani Ratnam started working later only at a time when she had already left, otherwise they could have created history together.

Mohan Raman: Yes, but she went there and, well now you're writing a book on her. You are a Bengali gentleman from the Northeast and you are writing about her—a Bombay star who came from Chennai. That honour came to her because she chose to shine in Hindi films...had she remained here, that might not have happened. For instance how many people know about Srividya, the other name I mentioned? The film aficionados, those who probably watch South films, only they would know. Sridevi then would have probably been stuck as a local legend. Today, she's a national treasure. So that way her decision made sense. Tamil film industry missed her. Everything about the film industry is like the cricket team. Sachin Tendulkar was a such a huge presence. When he left what happened? The team didn't stop playing, right?

AR: She shifted base completely. It was not even like Rajini or Kamal who were kind of shuttlecocking between here and Bombay... Not that it worked for them, commercially speaking.

Mohan Raman: Yes! That is where I think her wisdom came into play. She probably saw the success of others like Rekha who had to shift completely. Yes, Vyjayanthimala or Padmini were there, but that was in the '50s where they could operate in both the industries. But she knew that was not going to happen to her. So, the point is, she was learning from not just others' successes but others' failures also. She saw how Kamal was reluctant to move there for good, or Rajini was more here and forayed there. She saw all of that and decided if I have to go, I have to go. If I have to to stay, I have to stay. I can't be having the cake and eating it too.

So she was a brilliant student, learning not just from the successes but from the failures of others. That's what a good actor is. You watch your own performance and say, 'Oh my God, why did I lift my hand there? Why did I put my hand in the pocket there? Why did I rub my beard here? I shouldn't have.' You avoid it in the next film or the next time that such an opportunity presents itself. So, she learned from the successes of others—the way to choose roles like MGR or Sivaji, and when to shift [...] how to shift from the successes and failures which she saw. She, as I said, is probably the only person in contemporary cinema... and dare I probably say in the last 30–40 years, who was a successful, tremendously talented actor who said, 'Okay, now I need a larger stage. I have been the queen here, but it's a small stage.'

AR: And she was comfortable even there! She was so comfortable on-screen doing 'Hawa Hawai'! I was totally shocked when I saw *Moondru Mudichu*...when I was exposed to that body of her work. I was shocked—is this the same person?

Mohan Raman: Probably she subconsciously didn't want the same person to go. So that's why she changed the face of it. Maybe there was a battle going on inside. Look, she had to compete with terrific beauties. Towards the end of her career, I think, people like Madhuri had also come in. Rekha was always there. And Jaya Bachchan, Hema Malini were at the fag end of their career. Jaya Prada was also coming in around the same time. So there was a lot of competition, and all were what I would call classic beauties. Sridevi decided—okay, let me match them. She did not hesitate to dance toe-to-toe and box. She was like a boxer who was willing to play by the rules of that boxing match. You talk about World Heavyweight Championship—she will play accordingly. You say it's kickboxing, Thai boxing, she will play along. And if you say it's WWF—she'll play that. What she had was immense talent and potential and love for the craft, which means she loved being in front of the movie camera.

She loved her image being captured by it and relayed to millions of people. She loved the fact that they loved to see her. She enjoyed it. She revelled in it, it was her sustenance. It was the source of all her energies. The moment she knew that was her she didn't even hesitate for a minute to completely transform. Which is why she looks so comfortable during 'Hawa Hawai'. You can clearly see that some of the other actors, without mentioning names, are extremely uncomfortable in doing the masala-mushy romance. She was completely at ease...imagine that all-time classic rain song from *Mr India*. She was dancing with gay abandon!

Any woman would be conscious of the fact that this kind of a sari, when wet, will be a little transparent. She was living in the moment and that was, I think, her biggest asset. She was living in the moment.

AR: Interesting you mentioned that song from *Mr India*, 'Kaate Nahi Kat-te Ye Din Ye Raat'. If we were to visually juxtapose *Mr India*'s Sridevi dancing in the blue sari with Mayil in *Pathinaru Vayathinile* and the mother she played in *Moondru Mudichu*... She was like almost ageing backwards... and physically transforming into something else.

Mohan Raman: It was almost as if she was a caterpillar here and became a butterfly there. Child artist was the larva, Tamil actor was the pupa and the Hindi diva was the butterfly. But ultimately it is the same living being...she was so much at ease. That is the beauty of Sridevi in my opinion. In my opinion, no other actor in contemporary cinema has come close to doing that. Probably Padmini of Tamil cinema was comfortable when I've seen her do all these, but the masala cinema as we know it hadn't begun as yet. It was different, there were actresses like Nargis and Nutan. But this lady was able to go from A to Z. Most people went from D to

G or H to K. She went from A to Z and to come back to *English Vinglish* and then *Mom*.

AR: She also finally came after so many years in a Tamil film. She did *Puli*.

Mohan Raman: Yes...but I don't know...I think there was a lot of chopping in the film, editing wise. But it was again a comeback and to do an evil queen...

AR: There was fire in her eyes!

Mohan Raman: ...An evil, evil queen.

AR: If somebody would be at home and doing the chores, I mean guy or girl whatever and, you know, were not in arc lights for like 15 years or whatever, your skill sets get rusted at some level. And it's visible that it's a comeback and you're probably not as comfortable around that. But she was back in her element.

Mohan Raman: See, for a lot of us it's probably like playing cricket where you need net practice every day. For her it was like cycling.

AR: It was almost like muscle memory...and she just came back!

Mohan Raman: Just came back, that's what I said, it's just like cycling. Not cricket. To me at 60 plus, if we decide to play, my entire instinct knows that this is a ball I have to reach out and play towards mid-off because I have to put my foot there. My mind tells my body, 'Okay, reach out.' My body can't. I'm slower. By the time, my leg goes out there the ball has already passed. In her case, it was like cycling. She just had to get on the bike, take a few uncomfortable pedals—probably the first take or the second take. And then she started zooming. Because after that, it is as you said, muscle memory. For somebody who's been on front of the camera from a very young age, you can't just ignore those years of experience.

AR: I sometimes think that...as a human being, having a family and raising children were definitely important for her. But performing came as naturally to her as breathing or like, you know, going to the loo or eating. I think it was almost like that for her—acting in front of the camera.

Mohan Raman: Living in front of the camera. She was more comfortable living in front of the camera rather than off.

AR: I have heard that she didn't like to party. Kamal, Rajini everybody had their own society and drink or whatever, right? Somebody was a bit less flamboyant, somebody was a bit more flamboyant but she had zero social life. She didn't interact with anybody. She was an on-and-off actor— that's what I was told. She was 'on' on the set. As soon as the job was done she would just go home like any other office goer. No other social life. No mixing with anybody, no talking to anybody.

Mohan Raman: And social life in Chennai those days was different, the actor population was thinner. You didn't have the kind of pubs and discos which is common nowadays. The youngsters are able to do that...they can enjoy social life as well. Those days it was very, very uncommon.

AR: Even later on, when she joined Hindi cinema there also she was not as open and she didn't socialize.

Mohan Raman: Yes, you probably saw much less of her in the film parties than the others.

AR: Sridevi, Kamal and Rajinikanth were almost working together around the same time. All three of them in different degrees were kind of trying to make a name for themselves. I mean, either of the men were not a big star by that time. So, would it be right to say that Sridevi was the first among the three to become a popular actor? Did *Pathinaru Vayathinile* give her more advantage, than it did for Kamal. Kamal's role in *Pathinaru Vayathinile* reinforced part of what people already at some level knew—that he was a good actor. He was a solid actor. But was Sridevi kind of a revelation with *Pathinaru Vayathinile* and *Moondru Mudichu* and became a popular actress?

Mohan Raman: She was the first to cross the line. The line to mini stardom. I would reckon so because it took a lot of time. In fact, I would say that...both Rajini and Kamal owe their huge public persona to a director called S.P. Muthuraman [SPM].

AR: I thought it was more of K. Balachander.

Mohan Raman: Balachander created them, gave them the craft, did all that but he didn't make them mass heroes. It was S.P. Muthuraman who gave them the image. He is the only director who directed both Rajini and Kamal in 20 plus films. And he was the guy who gave both of them roles which... You know, Kamal had to do what Sridevi did from here to go to Bombay. Kamal had to do it with SPM films. Rajini was given all his hard looks and the punches and the gimmickry and everything...he was given a free hand by SPM. [...] It took S.P. Muthuraman films to take both of these guys and launch them to a level where they were known names in every street corner but *Pathinaru Vayathinile* did that to Sridevi. And you know by the time of *Johnny* she had really grown. Her maturing was much faster as a public star. She was big, she was really big. And you must also realize she didn't have much competition at the top, whereas when Rajini and Kamal were there you could say that Sivaji Ganesan was still active. Some of the senior actors were still active and slowly they had to conquer one by one and come up. Whereas, she literally had the field open. It was waiting for the swan to come and she came. In their case, there were other animals in the zoo. So, for them to become the star attraction they had to go loudest and then attract the attention. Whereas in Sridevi's case, the field was open. She just sort of breezed through at that point of time.

Afterword
by Ram Gopal Varma

I first witnessed the angel called Sridevi in a darkened theatre in Vijaywada. The film was *Padaharella Vayusu* and I was awestruck by her beauty, grace, charm and talent. She was the epitome of perfection for me. I was so preoccupied with her beauty that it took numerous films for me to recognize the actress in her. This acting prowess was showcased in many South Indian films but most effectively in the Tamil film, *Moondram Pirai*.

I had the privilege of working with her on two films, *Kshana Kshanam* and *Govinda Govinda*. Both were thrillers that showcased her versatility and charisma. She could play any role with ease. Whether it was comedy, drama, action, romance or dance, she had a natural flair. She was the complete package.

When we were shooting for *Kshana Kshanam* at Nandyal, a crowd of more than 10,000 people surrounded her bungalow all through the night just to get one look at her. She had to be guarded at all times by some local toughies and at least 100 policemen. It was easy for us to know that she was headed for the location from her bungalow owing to the column of dust that travelled towards us, caused by the countless people chasing her car. It was incredible.

Sridevi was the most beautiful and desirable woman ever, for millions of her fans. She was also the biggest superstar in the country and ruled the silver screen for decades. She faced multiple hardships in her life and career, as I came to know later. She was living proof of how a star's real life can be very different from how the fans perceive it. As she joined this career very early on as a child artiste, life never gave her time to grow up like a normal kid. To the world, she came across as a little uptight and reserved because of the walls she had built around her. Sridevi was truly an enigma.

But behind this mesmerizing façade lay a woman of immeasurable strength and resilience. Sridevi's journey through life was rife with trials and tribulations. Yet she emerged triumphant, time and again. With every setback, she reinvented herself—rising from the ashes like a phoenix, stronger and more radiant than ever before. Her tenacity and unwavering spirit serve as an inspiration to all those who dare to dream, a testament to the power of perseverance and self-belief.

For me, Sridevi was not merely an actress. She was an inspiration, a dream, a fantasy, a goddess. Just like in the film *Jagadeka Veerudu Athiloka Sundari,* she was a celestial being sent to grace our mortal realm with her ethereal presence. Her name shall forever be etched in the hallowed halls of cinema, serving as a beacon of inspiration for generations to come. I am an atheist. I do not believe in reincarnation or rebirth. But for her sake and the sake of her fans, I want to believe that she will be born again. All of us fans, we deserve to experience her once again in our next birth. But then, we will try our best to make ourselves worthy enough to deserve her.

I congratulate Amborish Roychoudhury for writing *Sridevi: The South Years* and honouring Sridevi's contribution to South Indian cinema. I hope that this book will be read by Sridevi fans and admirers the world over. I believe it will move and inspire them to watch or re-watch her films, and appreciate her talent and breathtaking beauty. I hope it reminds them of why they loved Sridevi, and why they still miss her.